The Lazy Pro

*How to be twice as productive and
still leave the office early*

PETER TAYLOR

*To David, my manager and mentor for the last
fifteen years, who has actively encouraged my laziness
at all times.*

*And to my family, whose increasing demands for
money have driven me, not to drink, but to authorship
and public speaking.*

Thank you.

Peter Taylor

The lazy project manager

*How to be twice as productive and
still leave the office early*

infiniteideas

First published in 2009 by
Infinite Ideas Limited
36 St Giles
Oxford
OX1 3LD
United Kingdom
www.infideas.com

A CIP catalogue record for this book is available from the British Library

ISBN 978-1-906821-67-8

Designed and typeset by Kerry Pearson
Printed and bound by TJ International Limited, Cornwall

Contents

Acknowledgements

I have received a lot of support during this project, the writing of my first book, and I want to thank everyone.

I will avoid doing it by name (you all know who you are), but I will do it by role instead – this will both help protect the guilty and keep me safe from forgetting someone important.

There was my flight companion back in 2008 who, when asking me what I wanted to do next in my career, declared that being an author and public speaker was a great idea but that I was probably too lazy! Well, that was the catalyst, for sure.

There were those who didn't laugh (too much) when I put together the idea for the lazy project manager and the first version of the website (www.thelazyprojectmanager.com) and bravely showed it to other people for the first time.

And there were those who supported me during the writing period itself, commenting, and contributing, reviewing, acting as unpaid editors and generally helping out.

Finally, thank you to Richard at Infinite Ideas for having nothing better to do on the day my book idea landed in his in-box.

Thanks to all of you.

Introduction

Productive laziness is all about success, but success with far less effort.

By advocating being a 'lazy' project manager, I do not intend that we should all do absolutely nothing. I am not saying we should all sit around drinking coffee, reading good books and engaging in idle gossip whilst watching the project hours go by and the non-delivered project milestones disappear over the horizon. That would obviously be just plain stupid and would result in an extremely short career in project management – in fact, probably in a very short career, full stop!

Lazy does not mean stupid.

No, I really mean that we should all adopt a more focused approach to project management and exercise our efforts where it really matters, rather than rushing around like busy, busy bees involving ourselves in unimportant, non-critical activities that others can better address, or which do not need addressing at all in some cases.

Welcome to the home of 'productive laziness'.

On the following pages you can read more about what I mean about productive laziness and how you can apply these simple techniques and approaches in your own projects. The major project topics will be covered but from a 'productive lazy' point of view.

I am not, by nature, a lazy person but I do have many other things to do in life, beyond the projects and programmes[1] that I manage, and I have therefore learned the manner in which to balance life, projects and work. What I am, though, and also by nature, is success orientated. Therefore the balanced approach that I utilise also has to ensure that both my projects and my career are successful and that they leave me with sufficient time for home and family. I am a Lazy Project Manager. You can carry on as you are or you can join me in the comfy chair of life and still get the project results that you and your project sponsors demand. Lazy does not mean unsuccessful.

It is, however, important to be clear what this concept of productive laziness is all about and, in the importance of scope definition, precisely what it is not about.

This is not a project management training manual. It will wholeheartedly fail to teach you to become a project manager; if you do want to learn about critical path analysis, earned value management, 'Monte Carlo' simulation, work breakdown structures, critical success factors and terms of reference then put this book back down and pick up an (allegedly) more boring-looking one that is no doubt somewhere nearby. You can come back to my more interesting book later on when you need a little light refreshment for the mind.

Equally, it is not a replacement for a good fundamental project management education programme. There are, I guarantee, huge parts of the project management skill set and process missing.

1. Programme management or program management is the process of managing multiple interdependent projects that lead towards an improvement in an organisation s performance. It typically supports a strategy in place for the business, such as an ambition to be the fourth biggest supermarket by 2015 or reduce wastage by 5% in two years.

It is not an alternative to a project management methodology; definitely not. And it is not a replacement for experience or for valuable support from an experienced project management coach. All these things you should already have in place, achieved or secured – or, if not, have a plan in place in order to do so.

But it is a sharing of my experience and can act, to some degree, as a virtual coach for you in your project work. It does describe a way to 'work smarter'. It is, if applied well, a means to become more productive in what you do for your projects and what you can do outside your projects. It can deliver a better work–life balance.

It works, and has worked, for me and it may work for you as well. I hope so. To be clear again, I have been formally trained in many project management methodologies over the years, I am a certified PMP® through the Project Management Institute (PMI)[2], and I have obviously had a lot of practical experience over the last twenty years in a wide range of projects and businesses and have been supported by some great project managers in my time.

Being a Lazy Project Manager is all about being focused in your project management efforts and learning to exercise your efforts where it really matters, where they make the most impact.

---

2. The Project Management Institute (PMI) is a non-profit professional organisation dedicated to advancing state-of-the-art of project management. It is the world s leading association for the project management profession. PMI sets standards, conducts research, and provides education and professional exchange opportunities designed to strengthen and further establish professionalism. This institute aims to advance the careers of practitioners and enhance the performance of business and other organisations. This is done by running and maintaining five credentials in project management including the 'Project Management Professional which is properly expressed as the credential PMP .

There are many, many books that will take you into every detail of every component of the project management skill set and process steps; this is not one of them. This is project management from 37,000 feet. So welcome to the project management 'mile high' club!

The science behind the laziness

This isn't all just made up you know, there is science and history and a singing bear behind all this theory.

The Pareto principle (also known as the 80/20 rule) states that for many phenomena, 80% of the consequences stem from 20% of the causes. The idea has a rule of thumb application in many places, but it's also commonly misused. For example, it's a misuse to state that a solution to a problem 'fits the 80-20 rule' just because it fits 80% of the cases; it must be implied that this solution requires only 20% of the resources needed to solve all cases.

The principle was in fact suggested by management thinker Joseph M. Juran and it was named after the Italian economist Vilfredo Pareto, who observed that 80% of property in Italy was owned by 20% of the Italian population. The assumption is that most of the results in any situation are determined by a small number of causes.

So '20% of clients may be responsible for 80% of sales volume'. This can be evaluated and is likely to be roughly right, and can be helpful in future decision-making. The Pareto principle also applies to a variety of more mundane matters: we might guess – approximately – that we wear our 20% most favoured clothes about 80% of the time; perhaps we spend 80% of the time with 20% of our acquaintances, and so on.

The Pareto principle is unrelated to Pareto efficiency, which really was introduced by Vilfredo Pareto. Vilfredo Pareto (born 15 July 1848 in France, died 19 August 1923 in Lausanne, Switzerland) made several important contributions to economics, sociology and moral philosophy, especially in the study of income distribution and in the analysis of individuals' choices. He introduced the concept of Pareto efficiency and helped develop the field of microeconomics with ideas such  as indifference curves. In 1906, he made his observation about Italian property which was later generalised into the Pareto principle, and into the concept of a Pareto distribution.

The Pareto principle or 80/20 rule can and should be used by every smart but lazy person in their daily life. The value of the Pareto principle for a project manager is that it reminds you to focus on the 20% that matters.

Woody Allen once said '80% of success is showing up'. I'm not so sure about that; I have seen projects where there was a physical project manager around, but you would never have believed that looking at the project's progress, or lack of progress. No, it's better – I believe – to appreciate that out of all the things you do during your day, only 20% really matter. Those 20% produce 80% of your results. So you should identify and focus on those things during your working day.

Do this well and you will enjoy the world of productive laziness.

The intelligence of laziness

It's no good just being lazy; you have to be better than lazy, you have to be lazy in a very smart way.

Productive laziness is not just about being lazy, it requires something more – and that is a powerful and magical combination of laziness and intelligence. Smart lazy people have a real edge over others in society and are most suited to leadership roles in organisations. This theory has existed for many years and has been applied in a number of interesting ways. One of the most famous of these was in the Prussian Army.

Helmuth Karl Bernhard Graf von Moltke (26 October 1800 – 24 April 1891) was a Generalfeldmarschall. He is widely regarded as one of the great strategists of the latter half of the 1800s, and was the creator of a new and more modern method for directing armies in the field.

In 1857 Helmuth von Moltke was given the position Chief of the Prussian Grosser Generalstab (military staff), a position he held for the next thirty years. As soon as he gained the position he went to work making changes to the strategic and tactical methods of the Prussian army – changes in armament and in means of communication, changes in the training of staff officers and changes to the method for mobilising the army. He also instituted a formal study of European politics in connection with plans for campaigns which might become necessary. In short, he rapidly put into place the features of a modern General Staff.

Moltke had a particular insight and approach to categorising his officer corps, something which lives on to this day within many armed forces, and something which can be applied to all forms of leadership, including project management.

If you consider the two ranges of individual characteristics, those that go from diligent through to lazy, and those that go from non-smart through to smart (yes, I am being politically correct here), then you end up with the four character types in the diagram below.

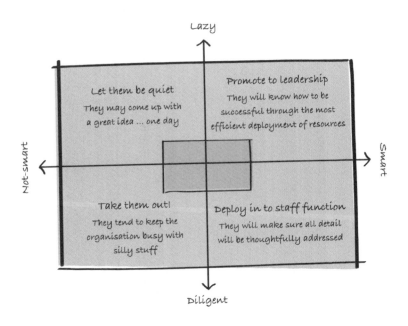

General von Moltke divided his officer corps into these four distinct types, depending on their mental and physical characteristics. He ended up with (and he never had to be politically correct, having been born in the nineteenth century and being chief of the Prussian army) type A: mentally dull and physically lazy; type B: mentally bright and physically energetic; type C: mentally dull and physically energetic; and type D: mentally bright and physically lazy.

Type A officers, who were mentally dull and physically lazy, were given simple, repetitive and unchallenging tasks to perform. They had reached their career peak in the army. That said, if left alone they might just come up with a good idea one day; if not, then they wouldn't cause any problems.

Type B officers, who were mentally bright and physically energetic, were considered to be obsessed with micromanagement and would, as a result, be poor leaders. Promotion was possible over a period of time but not to the status of commanding officer of the General Staff. These officers were the best at making sure orders were carried out and thoughtfully addressing all the detail.

Type C officers, who were mentally dull but physically energetic, were considered to be somewhat dangerous. To Moltke, they were the officers who would require constant supervision, which was an unacceptable overhead and distraction. Because they would potentially create problems faster than could be managed, these officers were considered too much trouble and were dismissed. No career there, then!

Which brings us to type D officers. These were the mentally bright and yet physically lazy officers who Moltke felt could and should take the highest levels of command. These officers were smart enough to see what needed to be done but were also motivated by inherent laziness to find the easiest, simplest way to achieve what was required. Put in a more positive way, they would know how to be successful through the most efficient deployment of effort.

'Whenever there is a hard job to be done I assign it to a lazy man; he is sure to find an easy way of doing it.

Walter Chrysler

OK, now take your pick. What do you want to be? Type A, B, C or D? Tough question, eh?

So, smart lazy people have a real edge over others and are most suited to leadership roles in organisations. The Lazy Project Manager is all about applying these principles in the delivery and management of projects. It is assumed that you are not stupid (well, you have bought or borrowed this book and I see that as a positive sign of intelligence), so you are already on the right hand side of the diagram. What you now need to do is hone your lazy skills in order to rise to the top right hand side of the diagram. Do this, and not only will your projects be more successful, you will also be seen as successful yourself, and a safe pair of hands for future leadership roles.

A final definition

It's a kind of magic: when one plus one equals so much more than two.

So what do you get when you cross one of the seven deadly sins (sloth – number four in the modern-day listing, as it happens) with an accelerant for resource usage (good old productivity)?

- **lazy** [leizi]   adjective (lazier; laziest)

1. If someone is **lazy**, they do not want to work or make any effort to do anything.

    – **Lazy** and incompetent workers are letting the company down.

    – I was too **lazy** to learn how to read music.

- **laziness** noun

    – Current employment laws will be changed to reward effort and punish **laziness**.

2. You can use **lazy** to describe an activity or event in which you are very relaxed and which you do or take part in without making much effort.

    – Her latest novel is perfect for a **lazy** summer's afternoon reading.

    – We would have a **lazy** lunch and then lie on the beach in the sun.

- **lazily**   adverb

    – Lisa went back into the kitchen, stretching **lazily**.

3.　If you describe something as **lazy**, you mean that it moves or flows slowly and gently.

　　– ...a valley of rolling farms spread out along a **lazy** river.

　　• **lazily**　　adverb

　　– The river threaded its way **lazily** between the old city and the new.

Laziness – sloth: apathy and inactivity in the practice of virtue (personified as one of the deadly sins).

So lazy – or laziness: is mostly seen as a negative term, or at the very best, as a term of selfish indulgence.

Productiveness – on the other hand, is seen as a very positive term: the ratio of work produced in a given period of time. Productivity relates to a person's ability to produce the standard amount or number of products, services or outcomes as described in a work description.

So, put the benefits of productiveness together with an intelligent application of laziness and you get 'productive laziness'.

Or, to put it another way, you get the maximum output for any given input, with an eye to minimising the input as well. Or, to put it yet another way, you get a lot of bang for your buck, as some like to say!

It s a jungle (book) out there!

Doo be doo be doo: inspiration from a great 'character' actor.

You know that scene from *The Jungle Book,* one of Disney's great films[3], where the bear Baloo encourages Mowgli, the boy, to think about life in a different way?

Baloo sings about looking for just the bare necessities of life, about trying to relax and cool it, and not spending any time looking for things that aren't worth it or can't even be found. Or, put another way, he is explaining to Mowgli that life using the good old 80/20 rule can be a lot less stressful.

For me 'The Bare Necessities' could well be the productive lazy theme tune. Check out the full lyrics some time, take a stroll down memory lane and watch the film one more time and enjoy Baloo the (singing) bear teaching you all about the bare necessities of life that will come to you.

If that isn't good old doo be doo be doo productive laziness, I don't know what is!

---

3. The Jungle Book is an animated feature film, released on 18 October 1967. The nineteenth in the Disney animated features canon, it was the last to be produced by Walt Disney, who died during its production. It was inspired by the stories about the feral child Mowgli from the book of the same title by Rudyard Kipling. The movie remains one of Disney s most popular, and contained a number of classic songs, including 'The Bare Necessities' and 'I Wanna Be Like You . Most of the songs are by Richard M. Sherman and Robert B. Sherman.

Can I cheat?

It is impossible for a man to be cheated by anyone but himself[4], so it's your call entirely…

So you are already thinking in the 'lazy' way? That combination of inherent intelligence and underlying laziness is kicking in already?

You are wondering if you really have to read the whole book through, study the contents carefully, connect with each idea and experiment in your daily project life in order to reach the higher plane of conscientiousness that is productive laziness. You are thinking that this seems like an awful lot of hard work considering this book is supposedly teaching you to take it easy in the comfy chair.

Or maybe you are one of those people who just have to skip to the end and see what happens. Or maybe you want to just validate the value of the book before investing any more of your overly hard-worked-for money by seeing some sort of summary and conclusion.

Possibly you are a student of project management who, having left some piece of work right to the very last moment – again – is rushing to grab as many salient points and quotes on this subject as possible, with as little actual effort as possible, in order to both meet a deadline and achieve an acceptable grade.

---

4. 'It is impossible for a man to be cheated by anyone but himself.' Ralph Waldo Emerson (1803–1882).

Whatever the reasons, and in the extremely selfish interests of a potential book sale, here is the answer you are looking for:

Yes!

Yes, you can cheat. Yes, you can skip all the way to the chapter which is entitled 'Quick tips to productive lazy heaven'. And, yes, there you will find what you are looking for.

But – just before you head off to the end of the book – I do hope that you will return to the next chapter at some point, partly because it does set the scene for the structure of the book (and the quick tips), partly because there are many wise words and ideas covered that will help you in the future, and also partly because I have spent a long time writing this book and will probably sulk if you don't.

OK, decision time. See you on the next page – or later on, near the end of the book.

The dinosaur theory

Richard Owen[5] may have got it wrong; here's an alternative view to the traditional one...

This book is structured around a particular theory that I have. It is my theory and no one else's and it goes like this. Are you ready?

Good. Here we go, then.

Theory by Miss Anne Elk:

'All brontosauruses are thin at one end, much, much thicker in the middle, and then thin again at the far end. That is my theory, it is mine, and it belongs to me, and I own it.

Monty Python

5. The taxon Dinosauria was formally named in 1842 by English palaeontologist Richard Owen, who used it to refer to the 'distinct tribe or sub-order of Saurian Reptiles' that were then being recognised in England and around the world. The term is derived from the Greek words deinos meaning 'terrible', 'powerful' or 'wondrous' and saura meaning 'lizard' or 'reptile'.

**The Lazy Project Manager s theory of projects,
from a productive laziness aspect:**

'All projects are thick at one end, much, much thinner
in the middle and then thick again at the far end.

Thick at the end

Thick at the start

The point here is that, working by the productive lazy rule, a smart project manager should apply time and effort at the critical stages of a project, i.e. the start and the finish, and less time in the middle or the less critical stage. At this stage there are other people in the project who should be doing most of the hard work, and you probably deserve a bit of a rest anyway.

I do have a second theory (as did Miss Anne Elk,[6] by the way):

'If you want to get a brontosaurus from "a" to "b" then you ride the dinosaur – you don't carry it!'

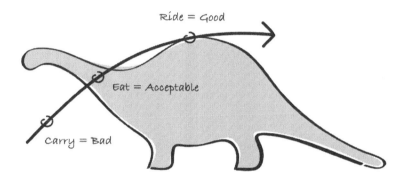

And the point, this time, is that as a smart project manager you should be directing the project and not trying to pick it up and carry its heavy, heavy load on your back all the way to the delivery gate. That way only failure, backache and heartache lie.

---

6. 'Anne Elk's Theory on Brontosauruses' is a sketch from the thirty-first Monty Python's Flying Circus episode. This features Graham Chapman as a television interviewer and John Cleese in drag as the palaeontologist, Anne Elk, appearing in a television talk show titled 'Thrust'. The plot of the sketch is that the interviewee, Anne Elk, cannot bring herself to describe the actual basis of her supposed new palaeontological theory on dinosaurs, specifically Brontosauruses. Ms. Elk spends most of the interview circuitously leading up to the 'theory of dinosaurs by Anne Elk', and making assertions like 'My theory, which belongs to me, is mine . It turns out that in the end Miss Elk s new theory on brontosauruses is rather shallow: 'All brontosauruses are thin at one end, much, much thicker in the middle, and then thin again at the far end.

The following chapters of this book lay out suggestions for ways to apply the 80/20 rule in your projects so that you can 'work smarter' and enjoy the rewards of productive laziness. It should also be remembered that it is as much to do about what you don't 'do' as to what you do 'do'. Do the things that will contribute to the 80% and avoid doing the things that won't.

We start at the beginning, of course, where the Lazy Project Manager's theory of projects, from a productive laziness aspect, states that 'All projects are thick at one end...'

Thick at one end

Where do you begin and with what, and after that what next?

So what is it that 'lazy' project managers should focus on during this initial 'thick' front end to their projects? And by front end – if you happen to be following, this is real project management terminology – then I am referring to initiation of the project. Well, the back end of initiation anyway. There is a project, you are the project manager, and the project is kicking off. Like I said: the thick front end.

So what is it that should get you out of the comfy chair and rushing into action?

Firstly, getting ahead, and then staying ahead, of the game. Then planning a strategy for managing the two critical players in any project – the project sponsor, who should be known at this point, and the project creep, who will be unknown but could be anyone or everyone, including, if you are really unlucky, the project sponsor, or, if you are really stupid, you.

And finally, the project manager needs to be planning for zero communication breakdowns, a singularly significant activity since general guidance suggests that some 70% of your time as a project manager should be spent in some form of communication or other.

'A bad beginning makes
a bad ending.

Euripides (484 BC   406 BC)

Three areas to focus on to ensure the project – that is, your project – starts off in the right way, in the right direction, and with the right momentum, and with the right processes and controls in place.

There is a well known project maxim that says 'Projects don't fail at the end. They fail at the beginning.' Failure at the beginning is just harder to spot and hurts a lot less – for a while, at least.

Ahead of the game

Start the way you mean to carry on and carry on the way you mean to finish.

Typically, when a project manager arrives at the start of a shiny brand new project then they will enter a point in time that is full of peace and love and general well-being between all parties involved. The sales cycle will be out of the way, if external suppliers are involved; the celebration parties will still be fond memories with people enthusiastically sharing embarrassing photographs on intranet sites, and everyone will believe that this is going to be a fantastic success with riches for all involved just around the corner. This project will be different from all the other projects.

Chaos reports[7] will be relegated to waste bins and the world will be a smiley happy place with optimism abounding. But we all know the reality of project history and the typical phases that projects experience:

- Enthusiasm

- Total confusion

- Disillusionment

- Search for the guilty

- Punishment of the innocent

- Reward and promotion of the non-participants

Obviously you want to avoid this scenario; you want to be a success. This is not, therefore, a time for a project manager to indulge in laziness; this will come later. No, for now, this is a time when project managers will be busy and visible and will stamp their authority on the project right from the very first moment, the very first phone call, the very first meeting, and the very first time they step into the project office.

It is at this point that the project can be won or lost for project managers, because it is now, and only now, that they will have the opportunity to drive and structure the project in the way they want to.

---

7. The Standish Group regularly produces CHAOS reports which research the reasons for IT project failures in the United States.

It's important to let everyone know that you have arrived and that you demand that things are done your way, the right way, the way that is best for the project. Equally, it's important that you educate your project team on why this is required and what benefits can be achieved by working your way – for them, for you and for the project. Productive laziness will follow, but for now take control and work hard. Now you need to understand exactly what you have taken on, or been landed with if this project was not actively selected by you. Now you need information and you will have many questions to ask and many answers to uncover.

And one word of warning before we start: there is a project management 'law' that says 'Attempts to get answers early in a project fail as there are many more wrong questions than right ones. Activity during the early stages should be dedicated to finding the correct questions. Once the correct questions have been identified, correct answers will naturally fall out of subsequent work without grief or excitement and there will be understanding of what the project is meant to achieve'. This is known as Hoggarth's Law.

Wise words, indeed; I think Hoggarth had the makings of a lazy project manager. Do not waste time – be productive, but in a 'lazy' way.

APPLYING THE PRODUCTIVE LAZY APPROACH

Start as you mean to go on

This means you should begin any new enterprise by acting and sounding as if it was already a success and by setting the standards you both expect and need to make that enterprise a success. In this case, your project is the enterprise and you have every intention of making a success of it. Non-negotiable; this is what it will be and failure is not an option. Your very attitude as you assume control for this change process will inform others that they are joining a winning team and setting out on a journey that will end in a sunset of success.

Confidence does breed success

Show you mean business by ensuring that all parties involved in the project both understand what you need and expect from them and also in what format you expect it – whether this is information, time, support, guidance or money. Not in an aggressive way, but in an authoritative way.

As part of this process it is equally important to explain to people why it is in their interest to deliver what you ask and to deliver it in the manner in which you request. Time now for some education, if needed, on what is good for the project is also good for the project team members.

Dress for success

Dress the part, as well. Even if you have people in your team that you have already worked with, make it clear at the start of any new project who the project manager is. Dressing to show this can help present your status and, therefore, your authority. Now, I am not suggesting building yourself a small throne in the project office and putting on a nice ermine cloak with a crown or anything crazy like that. No, just dress smartly and behave correctly. It is surprising, even in a casual working environment, how putting on a suit and tie (male) or smart suit and blouse (female) can adjust your attitude in a positive way. Maybe try it once a month if it is not the norm, or use it for steering meetings – whatever you feel is appropriate.

Get the upper hand

Getting the upper hand is always a great start to any project (in a nice way, or in a less than nice way if you have to). Not everybody will accept your authority at the very start of a project. A good way to gain the upper hand is to ensure that the people you may already have identified as being those who might give you some problems have deliverables very early on in the project. Now, if they should perhaps happen to be challenging deliverables that, maybe, they don't deliver on then you might say 'all the better'. If they fail, then they are the naughty ones from the very start of the project. Don't let them escape from their commitments or expected deliverables. I'm not saying set them up – not in so many words, anyway – but take opportunities as you see fit and use your experience to your advantage. Add to that maybe a few deliverables that are easy for you and your team to deliver and then you have the upper hand, for sure. Quick wins can be good things for you.

Another way to make sure that your authority is not challenged is to be prepared – like the boy scouts of your childhood – and be ready. Have that all-purpose penknife handy; you know, the one with the thingy that gets stones out of horses' hoofs. Well, at least have the project management equivalent of a Swiss Army knife ready, cleaned and polished to hand just in case you need it.

Be prepared

Be prepared and know your facts. Ensure you know all the facts you can in advance – do some research and have it on hand ready to produce. Most people usually fail to prepare their facts; they dominate meetings and conversations through sheer force and reputation. If you know and can produce facts to support or defend your position, it's unlikely that anyone will have anything prepared in response. When you know that a situation over which you'd like to have some influence is going to arise, prepare your facts, do your research, do the sums, get the facts and figures, gather opinions and views and be able to quote sources. Then you will be able to make a firm case, and also dramatically improve your reputation for being someone who is organised and firm, someone who is in control and who should be listened to and respected.

Anticipate everything you can

Also try anticipating other people's behaviour and prepare your own responses accordingly. This is not so easy at the start of a project, as often you will not know the characteristics of the people involved. But you can prepare your responses according to the possible different scenarios that you think could be presented to you. Make sure your close project team are with you on this, as well. You are not alone in all of this so involve the resources you have to hand and listen to what they have to say. Use them to help secure the position of strength and dominance that you want at this critical stage.

Don't just anticipate the people side of the project; anticipate what you can about the technical side, the business side, any external influences, anything and everything you can. Spending some time just thinking through the project timeline and considering possible issues or risks that may occur is a very productive thing to do. By imagining what might happen and then considering what could happen to avert or reduce that issue or risk will put you in a good position for if – or when – it does happen. It's just like a chess player thinking many moves ahead.

Being well prepared will increase your perceived confidence and enable you to be assertive about what's important to you.

Know the end game

Throughout this busy start up of the project it is critical that you both know and understand the end game or the final expected deliverables that your project is desired to achieve. Admittedly, many projects are still evolving these throughout the project initiation phase and, with the advent of more agile project methods these days, these deliverables evolve (to a certain extent) throughout the project lifecycle. But the end game must be watched like a light at the end of the tunnel or a beacon on the shoreline. Distraction from the end point of the project will impact your ability to make critically correct decisions along the way, crucial ones at the very start of the project, and your ability to direct the project in a steady and true path.

I guess this all sounds like a lot of work and somewhat counter-intuitive for the whole productive lazy theme. Well, believe me, this is an investment that is both critical and one that will pay huge dividends as the project progresses; it will allow you to become that lazy project manager and sit back in that comfy chair. But get on the back foot now and the project will be running you from day two onwards; you will be carrying that dinosaur all the way to the end date. Conversely, get it right now and life will be so much easier for the rest of the project.

A PROJECT MANAGER'S TALE WHERE
FIRST IMPRESSIONS COUNTED (AGAINST ME)

As a young and inexperienced project manager I began working on a new project at a large company based in Scotland. My job was to do all those things that I had been taught on my recent project management course. A good course but, like most courses, a course based on theory and documented best practice. So I knew about kick-off meetings, sponsors and steering meetings, scope control, issue management, risk management and mitigation, work breakdown structures, budgetary planning and all those really important things.

What I didn't know was that there was so much more to being a project manager. What I did know was that I had a smart new suit and tie and an extremely practical and shiny new business case for all my future project files. I was ready.

I worked for a small software house and, as part of the sale to this customer, my company could recognise some revenue upon delivery and installation of the software. A technician who was installing the software was already on site but needed some sort of software patch to solve a problem.

So I left my offices, headed to the customer site, parked my car and, on the way to my first steering committee meeting, popped in to the IT department with the required tape[8] in my hand (my shiny new briefcase in the other, of course). Passing a group of people on the way, I quickly made my delivery and headed back to the main building and into the meeting room in plenty of time for my first steering meeting.

---

8. For you youngsters out there, a magnetic tape for data storage was wound on large (10.5 in/26.67 cm) reels. This de facto standard for large computer systems persisted until the late 1980s.

I was greeted by the chairman of the steering committee, a man I had passed only minutes before in the group outside as I made my way to the IT department. 'Who are you then?' he asked, and when I explained that I was the project manager, he laughed and said 'I thought you were just some techie who had got lost'.

Ouch, that hurt! All that training and preparation, not to mention the investment in the nice suit and briefcase, had gone completely to waste in a matter of seconds. You know, even though he seemed to say what he did in good humour, it took me at least another six months to win his confidence that I was both a real project manager and that I knew what I was doing and could be trusted. That first chance encounter had significant implications for me and all because the first impression was not what I had planned, all because I was carrying a computer tape and therefore looked like a techie.[9]

First impressions really count. Make yours count in the right way.

Manage the sponsor

How to control your greatest asset and potentially your biggest threat.

Critical to any project's success is having a good project sponsor, but, like the saying goes 'you can pick your friends but you can't pick your relatives' – and the same is true of project sponsors. So what makes a good project sponsor and how do you deal with the one you have just inherited for your project?

9. The author would like to acknowledge that some of the nicest people he has ever met were proud to be called techies and so this is not a bad thing at all.

The project sponsor is the key stakeholder representative for the project and provides the necessary support for the project manager with the primary responsibility of achieving the project objectives and benefits. An inappropriate choice of project sponsor can seriously impact the possibility of success of the project and provide you, the project manager, with an unwanted additional overhead.

Now you can't practically ask sponsors for a CV[10] and put them through a formal interview process, nice as it would sometimes be to utter the phrase 'I'm sorry, but I don't think this is the job for you right now'. But you should evaluate the sponsor you have and complete – in a subtle way, of course – a 'strengths and weaknesses' assessment so that you can adapt your project approach and communication methods to maximise their sponsorship support for the project that you now manage.

You can also openly discuss your intended plans for project management and communication to ensure that they fully buy into what you intend and how you intend to achieve it.

Responsibilities for project sponsors typically include:

* Providing direction and guidance for strategies and initiatives.

* Negotiating funding for the project.

* Actively participating in the initial project planning.

---

10. A CV, also called a curriculum vitae or a résumé, sometimes spelled resumé or resume, is a document that contains a summary or listing of relevant job experience and education. This is typically the first item that a potential employer encounters regarding the job seeker and is used to screen applicants, often followed by an interview, when seeking employment.

- Identifying project steering committee members.

- Working with the project manager to develop the project charter.

- Identifying and quantifying business benefits to be achieved by successful implementation of the project.

- Reviewing and approving changes to plans, priorities, deliverables, schedule, etc.

- Gaining agreement amongst the stakeholders when differences of opinion occur.

- Assisting the project when required (especially in an 'out of control' situation) by exerting organisational authority and the ability to influence.

- Assisting with the resolution of inter-project boundary issues.

- Chairing the project steering committee.

- Supporting the project manager in conflict resolution.

- Making the project visible in the organisation.

- Encouraging stakeholder involvement and building and maintaining their ongoing commitment through effective communication strategies.

- Advising the project manager of protocols, political issues, potential sensitivities, etc.

- Evaluating the project's success on completion.

The project sponsor should be a senior manager with the financial and organisational power to act quickly and decisively in the overall governance of the project. It is an active, hands-on role, requiring a supportive working relationship with the project manager and effective communication with major stakeholders. The project sponsor should have a broad knowledge of the business, including experience and expertise in the functional areas addressed by the project.

APPLYING THE PRODUCTIVE LAZY APPROACH

Ask them what they expect

It is important to get the project off to a good start and build a strong relationship with your project sponsor. Don't take any second-hand statements, references, quotes or rumours to be the truth about a project sponsor's views and expectations. Ask them. Clarify directly and only take their word for what they want and expect.

Now, it may well be possible that your sponsor may not yet know what they expect. It may be their first time as a project sponsor and the role could be as new to them as they are to you. If that is the case, you need to help and guide them in the responsibilities they may have.

Either way, consider your first meeting with the sponsor, new or not so new to the role, known or unknown to you from previous projects. What would it be reasonable to cover in such a meeting?

I joked that you couldn't practically ask sponsors for their credentials for the job and put them through a formal interview process. Indeed, more often than not, the project sponsor has been chosen by the business well before you have been selected as the project manager. But let's just assume that you can interview them; this could be fun.

'Tell me why you think you are the right person for this job?' Well, what skills are you looking for in a good project sponsor?

'What strengths will you bring to the role?' What are the strengths that would make your life as a project manager that much easier?

'What are your points of weakness and what action will you take to address these issues?' What weaknesses are you looking to avoid at all costs?

Manage the first meeting

In preparing for that first meeting (interview) with your sponsor you will need to understand that some sponsors will have a very fixed vision for the project and will tell you, and the rest of the project team, exactly what they want, when they want it and what will happen if they don't get what they want. Be cautious with these sponsors; their strength of purpose and character may challenge your interviewing skills. But it is still essential that you end up with the clarity of purpose that you need to run this project and work closely with the project sponsor.

Other project sponsors may have a vision that appears to be an undefined conceptual possibility developed with a small dose of delusion and aided (allegedly) with a hint of illegal substance abuse.

OK, then, your sponsor will be somewhere between the above extremes (if you're lucky). What should you be asking?

Ask the questions you need to ask

Consider the following key topics: business objective(s), anticipated impact of the project deliverables, expected quality standards, significant risks seen at this stage, key dates on the project horizon, key stakeholders (beyond yourself and the project sponsor), and any budgetary constraints that are likely. In addition, you need to learn what style of communication and relationship this particular sponsor expects from you.

As in the previous chapter, first impressions really count so do your preparation well. If you conduct a good, professional, confident first meeting with your project sponsor you will not only demonstrate your capability in a good light, but you will also provide a valuable service to the sponsor.

Open discussion works

'Tell me about the project we have.' Feel free to start the conversation in a simple way, with an open question, and then follow up with other questions that you need to ask in order to reach a suitable level of confidence in your understanding of those key topics – business objectives, anticipated impact of the project deliverables, quality standards, significant risks at this stage, key dates on the project horizon, key stakeholders and budgetary constraints.

One tip, here: you are only on an information-gathering exercise right now. I know I said take the project with a firm hand from day one, but as far as the project sponsor is concerned I would advise being a little gentle to begin with, at least until you understand what type of sponsor you are dealing with. You can put your firm grip in place and negotiate hard later on; right now, just learn and inwardly digest what you are told.

Now you need to go ahead and 'interview' the project sponsor. But what happens if your sponsor fails the interview? Consider first if remedial work can be put in place to help them 'raise their game', or alternatively, can you fill any deficiencies that you identify – either by process or resources? If the failure is significant, this will be a real project risk. I guess now only two options remain – this project ain't big enough for the both of you, and one of you is gonna to have to leave town.

Once the interview is out of the way maybe you can check their references, or perhaps the next step is to get them to complete a psychometric test…

Here's one simple test you could try, just to help you filter out the extreme cases (the answer is at the end of this chapter – don't look yet). This question may or may not help with profiling your project sponsor but at the very least it is great fun at a project team social gathering.

A young woman[11] goes to the funeral of her mother. There she meets a man whom she has never met before. She identifies him as the man of her dreams and immediately falls in love with him, but she never speaks to him. She has no idea who he is and no one at the funeral has ever met him before or who knows who he is. Two weeks later she kills her sister. Why?

11. It does not have to be a woman; gender plays no role in either this question or the answer.

Apply the power grid

But let's not be pessimistic, that isn't going to happen to you; you won't get an extreme example of a project sponsor and they won't fail the interview. So what's your next move? Well, perhaps you should consider the power base that your project sponsor has. Use the power grid below to assess your project sponsor, assess their rating of interest in this project from high to low and their actual power in the organisation, also from high to low.

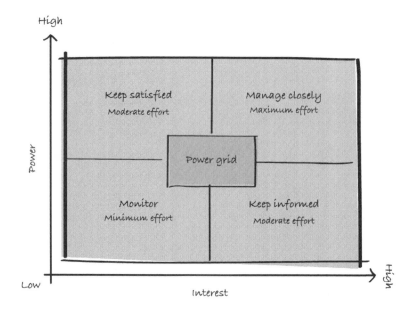

This will give you an indication of the way in which you should work with your sponsor. Actually this power grid is for all project stakeholders, and if you end up with a project sponsor that is in the 'low interest' and 'low power' quadrant you really have a problem. It is unlikely that this sponsor is ever going to support your management endeavours.

Types of power that count

Again for all stakeholders, but in particular for project sponsors, you need
to be aware that there are a number of types of power that can be present
in any organisation.

Where does your project sponsor fit?

* Legitimate – this can be through a formal title or position (authority).

* Reward – this can be through an ability to provide positive
  consequences for people (carrot).

* Coercive – this can be through the ability to provide negative
  consequences (stick).

* Purse string – this can be through budget control (money).

* Bureaucratic – this can be through knowledge of the system
  (intelligence).

* Referent – this can be through association with someone else's power
  (network).

* Technical – this can be through technical knowledge relating
  to the project (skill).

* Charismatic – this can be through personality alone (character).

Can you categorise your sponsor? Probably more than one from the above
list will apply, and that is a good thing.

Discover what s in it for them

Finally you need to understand what is in it for them – what their previous experience as a sponsor has been (both in their knowledge of being a sponsor and of real project experience, i.e. was a previous project a nightmare project?), if that is appropriate. Even if they have never 'sponsored' before they will no doubt have an opinion based upon stories they have heard about projects in the past.

And what's in it for you is the ability to work in that desired productive lazy management style but still deliver for your sponsor. Manage your sponsor well and you will have an ally in the coming weeks and months.

And now the answer to the question. Remember:

A young woman goes to the funeral of her mother. There she meets a man whom she has never met before. She identifies him as the man of her dreams and immediately falls in love with him. She has no idea who he is and no one at the funeral has ever met him before or who knows who he is. Two weeks later she kills her sister. Why?

Well, if you think in a very particular way, a way that indicates some potential as a psychopath (allegedly), then she killed her sister in the hope that the mysterious stranger at her mother's funeral would also attend the sister's funeral, since the only connection seemed to be with the family. By creating another critical family event, the woman may well see him again.[12]

---

12. I have only come across three people so far who have answered this question correctly (or incorrectly, depending upon your view of life). These people each responded almost instantly with the answer given here and were amazed that no one else could see this solution. Worryingly, one of these is my wife, Lisa.

A PROJECT MANAGER'S TALE WHERE SPONSORSHIP
WAS A FAST DISAPPEARING COMMODITY

I once attended a meeting, accompanying another experienced colleague, with a small group of three individuals in an English company. This company was very interested in initiating a business change project and engaged us to complete a project readiness assessment.

This assessment was a common service offering that ran over two days and allowed us to consider the state of 'readiness' of any company for a planned-for project. We would look at the business case, objectives and perceived project deliverables. We would consider risks and constraints. We would assess resources and management support for the project. And we would, at the end of the two days of interviews, go away and produce a project success plan outlining the project at a high level and indicating, through a 'traffic light' system, any areas of weakness in the project: red issues requiring mandatory action before commencing the project, and amber (orange) issues requiring action as early as possible in the project lifecycle.

So, we turned up on day one with the brief to interview 'the three sponsors of this project': the IT manager, the sales and marketing director and the operations director.

We were greeted by the IT manager and he laid out the bare bones of the project (this gave us some concerns as it immediately seemed to be an IT rather than business-led project, always a challenge). Anyway, we spent two hours with the IT man and then he took us off to meet the operations director.

It was a nice office with a big whiteboard, and up stood my colleague and outlined everything we knew about the project to be. Proudly turning to the operations director, confident in his professional style and ability to absorb and re-present information, he asked if he had 'missed anything'. 'Yes' came the solid reply. 'The point!'

It became clear, as the IT manager and the operations director began to argue – quietly at first and then more loudly – that there was almost no level of agreement between the two. Indeed, it seemed as if they had never even discussed this before. A red alert on our report was guaranteed. Eventually we were asked to leave the office and wait. We were shown a small area with a balcony where we could wait and so, on a fresh spring morning, we stared out over the balcony and waited. And waited. And waited some more.

Eventually we decided to head back to see if any common ground had been established, or whether one of the combatants had finished the other one off. But nothing. There was no one to be seen, anywhere. Confused, we managed to find ourselves back in the reception area and got a call through to the IT manager. Shaken and definitely stirred, he took us to lunch in the café and then pointed us in the direction of the sales and marketing director.

It was my turn to speak, so I stood up and repeated the position and understanding that we had had up to the start of the meeting with the operations director, and waited. Waited for a repeat of the last meeting. 'Looks really good,' came the response from the sales and marketing director. Naturally we, myself in particular, were enormously relieved. We were back on track.

Well, we were for all of two minutes!

'That said, I don't really care that much,' chuckled the sales and marketing director. 'I have just handed in my notice, resigned, so I won't be around.'

So we went from three project sponsors to none in one morning: one because he was leaving, one because he had no belief in or support for the proposed project, and one because he was just too weak and non-communicative to act as an effective project sponsor.

In the end it didn't matter that much. We delivered our report as best we could, and the project was never initiated.

Manage the creep

WATCH OUT, WATCH OUT, THERE'S A PROJECT CREEP ABOUT

It is not malicious and it is not planned, but the project creep is out there and will attempt to confuse your project, at the very least. The creep may be one person or many; they may have influence and authority or they may not; they may be in your project team or outside the team; they may be your ally or they may not. But what they will try and draw into the project, the project that you have so carefully planned, is change.

Project creep (as in functionality creep, feature creep, mission creep and scope creep) is a problem where the objectives of the project are put at risk by a gradual increase in overall objectives as the project progresses. So the project creep needs to be carefully managed, controlled, anticipated and dealt with.

Change, however, is good and the one thing you can be sure about on any project is that change will occur. So it is not change itself that we should fear but change in an uncontrolled manner and without thorough consideration for all the impact and consequences.

So beware the project creep. As a wise man once said many years ago 'Keep your project team close and the project creep closer'. Well, actually what he really said was 'Keep your friends close, and your enemies closer' and the 'he' was Sun-Tzu, a Chinese general and military strategist in about 400 BC and he said it in his book *The Art of War*, but you see what I am saying, I'm sure.

APPLYING THE PRODUCTIVE LAZY APPROACH

Creep is inevitable

The creep or creeps are out there and, in their mostly non-malicious way, they just want what is best for the business – which may, or may not, be what is best for the project. Remember, your job is to manage the project and deliver the agreed deliverables. Your job is to control the changes that are raised and support only those that are approved.

In general, the later a change is approved in the project lifecycle then the greater the impact cost will be. Gaps identified early on during the planning phase, through prototyping, simulation or any such means, can be evaluated and incorporated with a much lower level of additional investment than changes identified later on. And here I am not just referring to investments of cost.

Measure the creepiness

Why not see if you can profile your project team and assess the general 'creepiness' of your project? Use the creep'o'meter below (yes, another grid) to consider your colleagues and see if you can identify the hotspots for potential creep.

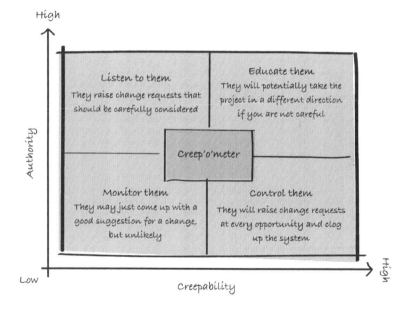

OK, so you have done that. What is the next logical step in the defence against scope creep?

Use the process

You have a change control process (well, I hope you have), so make sure that everyone, and I mean everyone, understands what it is, why it is there and how to apply it. Display it on the wall of the project office, print it on mouse mats, T-shirts, posters, anything that puts it in front of people as much of the time as possible. Then, when the very first change comes through, ensure that it goes through the change procedure absolutely, to the letter, without any deviation, and use this case as an example for all on the project to see.

Make it very visible to everyone how this first change request has been managed, where it is in the process, what decisions were taken and when, what the outcome is. Also explain the alternatives that could have occurred: if the change was rejected then what would have happened if it had been approved, and vice versa.

Manage the change

When is a change not a change? When you have educated people enough so that they don't even raise it in the system! Remember, your job is to deliver the project. Visionary concepts are not yours to dream; yours is the practical reality of delivering on time, at cost and to the agreed quality level.

Phrases no one on the steering committee will be pleased to hear include 'OK, we've had a little bit of scope creep. I don't know where it came from, but have you seen this cool little widget we've added…'

The use of more agile-based[13] project methods can also reduce scope creep. A key principle of Scrum[14], for example, is its recognition that during a project customers can change their minds about what they want and need (often called requirements churn), and that unpredicted challenges cannot be easily addressed in a traditional predictive or planned manner. As such, Scrum adopts an approach of accepting that the need cannot be fully understood or defined, focusing instead on maximising the team's ability to deliver quickly and responding to emerging requirements.

Park it in the parking lot

A great way to keep people happy is to say 'not now, later on…'. It occasionally even works with my kids.

The 'parking lot' is a means to record suggestions and requested changes, or even just ideas, in a particular place so they are not forgotten. People will be happier if they know that their great idea has not been forgotten or screwed up and thrown in the waste paper bin. If they can see you have duly noted and considered their idea and only deferred action until a later date (after this project phase) then they are less likely to complain and cause problems for you.

---

13. Agile methodologies generally promote a project management process that encourages frequent inspection and adaptation, a leadership philosophy that encourages teamwork, self-organisation and accountability, a set of engineering best practices that allow for rapid delivery of high-quality software and a business approach that aligns development with customer needs and company goals.

14. Scrum is an iterative incremental process of software development commonly used with agile software development. Despite the fact that 'Scrum' is not an acronym, some companies implementing the process have been known to adhere to an all capital letter expression of the word, i.e. SCRUM. Although Scrum was intended to be for the management of software development projects, it can be used in running software maintenance teams or as a programme management approach.

Park it but don t forget it

But don't forget that parking lot – you will have to do something with it at the end of the project. I would suggest including all the suggestions as a section of your project closure report. This way people will see their ideas as valuable contributions, and ones that have been properly managed by the project, by you and by their company. It will then be up to the project steering committee to consider them for a further phase of the project or reject them. The important thing is that this mechanism does not discourage people from raising suggested ideas, does not turn them against the project, does not clog up the change system with unnecessary change requests and, finally, removes you from the role of rejecter (if, indeed, that is the end result).

Thank them, thank them all

And finally, despite the varying levels of creepiness out there, despite what you might feel about the changes themselves and despite where you are in the project lifecycle, thank each contributor to the change register.

For sure, prepare them for what you expect, educate them in the process and the impact, persuade them to allow you to park their ideas in the parking lot but don't alienate them. They are, most likely, only trying to help.

A PROJECT MANAGER'S TALE OF WHEN NO DOESN'T REALLY MEAN NO

The project steering committee was a large one on a project I managed back in my early days of project management. There were, as there are in most projects, some real characters on the committee. One particular individual had a very specific attitude to this project, I was to find out, and a very determined intention. Yes, it was a project commissioned by the company as a whole but, as this person had, through his family, a particular connection with the founders of the company, he felt that he had a special relationship and authority.

Anyway, in the specification work that took place over a three-month period one particular piece of functionality was requested, investigated, reviewed and formally rejected after considered discussion. In general it was felt that this feature, neat though it might well be, was not crucial to the overall success of the project, nor was it overwhelmingly wanted by the intended users. And, as far as I was concerned, that was that. Move on.

And move on we did. The project was well underway when I happened to be in the rest area enjoying a coffee and some peace and quiet when the 'character' sat down opposite me. 'How's that work coming along on my request?' he asked.

Well, I was at first confused, but after some further conversation it became clear that he was talking about his pet requirement, the one that the steering committee had rejected. It was as if he had never been at any of those specification review meetings, never received or read any of the change communication and certainly wasn't in the meeting when this particular request was rejected. I explained the situation once more. 'Shame,' was the only reply I received, and I was left alone at the table with my coffee once again.

I put the conversation down to confusion on the other person's part and quickly forgot about it. I may, in fact, have rapidly moved my attention on to a nice piece of chocolate cake that I was enjoying with my coffee.

At the next steering meeting I had a moment of déjà vu when the two of us, in the period before the meeting proper started, had an almost identical conversation. The only difference was that the 'Shame' response was appended with an 'It would really help us if we had that, pity,' comment. Patiently, I explained the situation once more. That, sadly, was not to the end of it.

A similar thing happened over the next eighteen months at irregular intervals. Conversations would be struck, outside meetings, at the coffee machine, in the car park, on the way through reception, but it was never confrontational and never aggressive. It was always polite and with a sort of sad and wistful conclusion when each time I responded in the same way: 'Shame'.

It was like the goldfish in the goldfish bowl with the three second memory span.[15] 'Oh, look, a castle', swim, swim, swim; 'oh, look, a castle', swim, swim, swim; 'oh, look…' – you get the idea. Each time I explained the history, the process and the decision. Each time I would get the same response, more or less: 'Shame'.

Finally we reached acceptance testing and sign off by the steering committee.

Despite all of the formalities of the process that were in place, despite the signed specifications stored away, despite the contract locked away in legal, and despite all of my best efforts, approval was delayed until the 'special feature' that was so much wanted by my colleague was duly re-costed, developed, tested and accepted.

How did this happen? What did I do wrong?

For one thing, I was outmanoeuvered. The person in question managed to get the role of acceptance manager and that gave him a position of added power. Secondly, the same person had influence at the top that he utilised in order to get his own way, influence that outranked that of the project convention. I was also fooled by his calm demeanour, apparent patient acceptance each time I explained the position and apparent (repetitive) acceptance of what I was telling him.

---

15. Yes, I know, goldfish don't have a three-second memory span. Research by the School of Psychology at the University of Plymouth in 2003 demonstrated that goldfish have a memory span of at least three months and can distinguish between different shapes, colours and sounds. They were trained to push a lever to earn a food reward; when the lever was fixed to work only for an hour a day, the fish soon learned to activate it at the correct time.

This person represented a very special sub-set of the 'high authority – high creepability' group, focused on the one special change that seemed so important to him. Not to the business as a whole, but personally – to him. I was never going to win this one but perhaps I should have re-registered the change request and taken it through the process and in front of the steering committee a second time. I will never know. Perhaps if his attitude had been different, argumentative and demanding, then the situation might well have been dealt with much earlier. But it wasn't.

The project creep comes in all shapes and sizes, so beware.

Communication breakdown

Avoiding having a nervous breakdown and going insane

There is, to my mind, a great book – *Alpha Project Managers* by Andy Crowe[16] – which talks about 'what the top 2% know that everyone else does not' and it certainly identifies communication as a key area that top project managers excel at.

The book, based on a survey of 5,000 project managers, states in its findings that 'Good communication is comprised of more than how the message is delivered. The information itself, the method used, and the timing with which it is delivered all contributes to effective communication.'

16. Excerpts and ideas from this book are reproduced with kind permission of the author and the publisher, Velociteach.

Communication on a project is a two-way process. You are communicating out and you are receiving communication back at you, and the usual complexities of filters and noise typically confuse the process of giving and receiving clear, accurate and understandable information. Communication is also sequential, communicated through chains of people, which will add that 'Chinese whispers' effect – either intentionally or accidentally.

When you add to that the sheer volume of communication these days – email, phone calls (landline and mobile), written, presented, verbal and so on – then life can be very tough for project managers who need to learn what they need to learn and to share what they need to share.

I was taught a truth in my early project management days: reporting is not communicating! The fact that the critical facts and important truths are buried somewhere in a report that the right people may be in possession of does not, in any way, mean that they have received the message.

I have also learnt that to waste time and effort in 'defensive' and 'offensive' communication –typically email these days – is truly pointless and will distract the project manager from the real issues. I know that building an email trail which, to put it bluntly, 'covers your ass' is easy to do but far better results can come from directing those same efforts into really effective communication.

Effective communication is about isolating the critical information, utilising the optimum communication method for the person (or people) that you need to communicate with, and delivering that information at the appropriate time. I would also add that in order to ensure that you receive the right information back, you need to educate people on what information you need, how you would like to receive that information and when.

APPLYING THE PRODUCTIVE LAZY APPROACH

Communicate as others need you to communicate

'If you wish to persuade me, you must think my thoughts, feel my feelings and speak my words,

Cicero, the Roman orator and statesman, once said.

This whole book is really about communication, but this part specifically covers communication. And lazy project managers will think very, very carefully about what they need to communicate and how they need to communicate it, and why they are communicating what they are communicating. The general guidance is that some 70% of a project manager's time will be spent in communicating. That's 70%!

So, if you play the productive lazy game at all, and you only apply it in one area of project management, it makes blinding sense to do it here, in communication. This is by far the biggest activity and offers the greatest opportunity for time in the comfy chair. Imagine if you would be able to save some of that 70% of your time, how much more relaxed would you be?

Understand how communication works

Now, you can go and do your homework, you can read a book, you can attend a course, you can search online to your heart's content, and you will find lots and lots and lots of information about communication.[17] I really don't want to get too technical here but simply put, and just so that you have a basic understanding, here is a summary.

There is a source – someone/something sending out the information.

There is the medium – this is the means by which the information is sent. Maybe this is spoken or electronic (email, fax, web, etc) or through the telephone; maybe it is paper-based (letter, poster, memo, sticky note, etc), or it could be visual – an image – or a sound. It could even be silent through a look, a smell, body language, colours or the arrangement of text (numbers or letters).

Then we have what is known as the receiver – someone/something that is receiving the information.

And the final part of the process is feedback. The source will not know whether the communication that has been sent has been successfully received unless some sort of feedback is received (some action or change in behaviour).

---

17. Communication is the process whereby information is imparted by a sender to a receiver via a medium. Communication requires that all parties have an area of communicative commonality. There are auditory means, such as speaking, singing and sometimes tone of voice, and non-verbal, physical means, such as body language, sign language, paralanguage, touch, eye contact or the use of writing. Communication is defined as a process by which we assign and convey meaning in an attempt to create shared understanding. This process requires a vast repertoire of skills in intrapersonal and interpersonal processing, listening, observing, speaking, questioning, analysing and evaluating.

OK, got that, easy, eh? Well no, there is a little more (lots more if you study the topic properly)…

Communication is just not simple. There are lots of different types of medium by which to send information and the way that the receiver understands the information might be very different to the way intended. Most of us will have received a text message from someone that we took to mean something completely different from what was intended, for example, and the same can be applied to email.

On top of all that, there are actually barriers to communication that can add to the challenge of communicating in successful and clear way. These can include:

* Language (you are communicating between speakers of different languages or, if in the same language, there may be an imbalance in the level of those language skills or local dialects may be in place).

* Content (maybe there is some 'deep space' technical content involved or acronyms or just long words that not everyone understands. Another variant of this are the levels of knowledge and expertise of the sender and the receiver).

* Understanding or the lack of understanding of what the receiver wants or needs (how they wish to be communicated with and what they want to communicate).

* Feedback (there can be a level of inadequate feedback, or none at all – have you ever been on those long conference calls where nobody says anything apart from the speaker?).

- Emotion – your very mood can cause communication interference (if you are angry or upset).

- Quality of the information being sent.

- The medium used (resigning from your job by text is not advised, for example).

- Lack of trust or honesty in the source.

- Lack of attention from the receiver (maybe a matter of priority, the status of the source or just poor listening skills).

- Cultural differences.

There are so many that it is amazing that we can communicate as well as we do on a daily basis.

I often fail at this. For example, telling my three boys it is time for bed should be easy. 'Adam, Sam, Scott, time for bed' – job done. In reality, they will be watching the TV or on their laptops or playing their game machines, or more typically doing all three at the same time. I will be somewhere else in the house and they won't be listening anyway, and even if they did, they would be filtering me out because they don't want to hear this particular piece of information. And so it results in the message being sent many times, at varying ranges and volume (accompanied by increasing threats/incentives).

Be honest and be open

So, having solved all the above challenges in communication, I would suggest that in order to keep the levels of successful and productive communication high, it is very important that you are both honest and open in all of your communications. Even if you cannot share everything with others you can at least be open and say that this is the situation and describe why.

Be honest and keep your promises, do what you say you are going to do, deliver what you say you are going to deliver. Trust is critical. The lack of trust or honesty in the source (you) is, as we have already seen, one of the barriers to communication. But if you fail someone then they are not only likely to resist future communications, they are also less tolerant when it comes to understanding such communications.

And, finally, honesty in communication should also extend to not over-promising or overselling anything.

There is very good Swedish saying 'Sälj inte skinnet förrän björnen är skjuten' which roughly translated means 'Do not sell the skin before the bear is shot'.[18] What is the point in successfully communicating to someone and overcoming all of the challenges that this entails, only to communicate something that isn't even true?

18. At least that is what they tell me it means; knowing the Swedes it is probably more likely to be something odd that involves snow and sex. If so, then you have my apologies for inadvertently offending you; in this case it is best to just you use the English translation. On the other hand if the translation is correct then the Swedes have my apologies, lovely people and great snow.

Communicate in the modern way

Now I get started on the modern world. The world of emails and texts and electronic information, the world of mobile phones and BlackBerrys, the world of conference calls and webinars, the world of almost instant communication. Shouldn't it be easy these days?

Well 'yes' but also 'no', and the 'no' is mainly because of three factors. One is the massive increase in non-visual communication – email, text, phone, conference calls, etc – and the less visual activity (in both sending and feedback), the greater the risk of misunderstanding. We even try and compensate for this; think of the 'smiley' faces we add to emails and texts, for example. Second, there is an equally massive rise in the sheer volume of communication each day – how many emails do you get each and every day? And third, the speed of communication development means less time considering the receiver(s). In the days of letter writing far more time was put into constructing these forms of communication. How many times have you read something that you wrote some time later and thought 'I didn't mean that', or how many times have you copied someone in on an email without checking the email trail?

Effective but minimal communication is always recommended. So here are my top ten tips on being productively lazy when comes to communication:

1. Understand how people, individuals, each want to be communicated with and adjust your style to suit them.

2. Explain to people how you yourself want (need) to be communicated with (and why).

3. Prioritise communication targets (if you do get temporarily overloaded reduce your communication to this list).

4. Validate that the communication you are providing is working for the receiver – in particular, for critical information does written communication need to be supported by your spoken clarification?

5. Delegate by plan – you have a project team so you don't have to be involved in everything (decide what you can delegate ahead and make it happen).

6. Filter – what you do get; don't get involved in those communications that you don't have to and someone has just copied you in on, and delegate at every opportunity.

7. Delegate by action – as and when you get new topics of communication always consider who else can do this for you (and then enforce that delegation).

8. Enjoy the real benefits of self-resolution (I am not saying don't do your job but actually it is amazing how many 'issues' or 'questions' can be answered or resolved without you getting involved, so don't leap in immediately; give others a chance).

9. Don't get involved just because it sounds interesting – ask yourself 'do I want to get involved?' and then 'do I need to get involved?' and get involved only if you can answer 'yes' to both those questions.

10. And now on to email, lovely, lovely email – the features and functions of email programs are many but I personally feel this leads to many forms of abuse…

a. Firstly I would say don't just save it, but edit it, filter it, summarise it, store it – and don't store it in your email program, put the essence of what the email is about somewhere else for later reference. Typically I have less than twenty emails in total in mine at any time, but I get a lot of emails each day. By keeping the list low it is easy to see new mails coming in and to deal with them almost immediately, and I never feel overwhelmed this way.

b. Many people will disagree with me regarding emails but I personally find that 'If you have to scroll you have lost control' so you can forget all your fancy email rules and filters and the like. I would say just deal with them and move on.

c. And do yourself and everyone else a favour, don't copy people in just because you feel like it, don't create ever growing distribution lists, do remove people from email lists if you can (and why reply to all every time? It's not necessary), don't use blind copy, do remove email trails that are unimportant, and don't copy yourself on emails (if you do feel you need that sort of audit trail you are probably screwed anyway).

d. Last but not least, if you have to forward something to someone, think about it twice, read the entire email trail carefully, and then think about it one last time before pressing the 'send' button. Email is great, but use it wisely.

Communicate the communication plan

Every project should have a communication plan in place. Make sure that everyone knows what this plan is and how they should be contributing to it. Also, validate its effectiveness on a regular basis. If it needs amending do so – and let everyone know.

Reporting is not communicating

Another well-known project management law, Cohn's law, sums this up so well. 'The more time you spend in reporting on what you are doing, the less time you have to do anything. Stability is achieved when you spend all your time doing nothing but reporting on the nothing you are doing.'

Putting together fantastically accurate and detailed reports and sending them to anyone and everyone is most definitely not communicating. They won't be read – no one has the time or the interest to do this – and they won't be valued and worse, when they do contain project-critical information, they will be ignored. You are wasting your time.

A PROJECT MANAGER'S TALE OF THE PERILS OF COFFEE-MACHINE COMMUNICATION

Working for a Japanese company, I assumed the project management role some four months in to the project. There had been another project manager before me, a colleague who had decided to 'move on'.

Being a diligent and conscientious project manager, I sat down with the team and reviewed the plan and the schedule. It rapidly became clear that the project was going to be late, and instead of a 'go live' date of 1 February it was more likely that a date of 1 May was achievable.

Anticipating the discussion I was going to have to have with the customer's project manager first, and then the steering committee later, I dutifully researched and documented the reasons behind the slippage of three months. In all honesty, they were 95% down to the customer. What my predecessor had failed to do was to communicate these slippages in an appropriate way. I could find all the causes and consequences buried deep down in the copious project status reports (each one an average of twelve pages long!) but none of this had risen to the surface at recent project meetings or steering meetings, and this news was therefore going to be a bit of a shock.

So, fully prepared for my later meeting with the customer, I needed to go to see another customer just down the road. As I left I commented to my technical architect that I was off, would be back 3 p.m. and 'would give the bad news then'.

I left. I returned.

The first person I met on my return was my technical architect who cheerfully informed me that he had met the customer's project manager at the coffee machine earlier and had given him the news.

And the result? Well, I had a tough meeting, and never got the opportunity to present the facts of the situation and build up to the consequences in a proper manner. I was on the back foot from the moment I walked in the door, and I never recovered. I was also replaced on the project in a few weeks and the third project manager assumed control and delivered the project (on 1 May).

Our sins? We had failed to communicate from the start of the project in an appropriate way, and when there was bad news we communicated it in an inappropriate and casual manner without control or consideration. My failure was that I did not communicate well enough to my project team what I intended to do and why I wanted to do it that way, nor the potential consequences of not being able to do it like that.

Much, much thinner in the middle

Driving the project on autopilot, from the comfy chair.

The Lazy Project Manager's theory of projects, from a productive laziness aspect: 'All projects are thick at one end, much, much thinner in the middle and then thick again at the far end.'

The Lazy Project Manager now oversees the project work with as light a touch as possible. The planning was done at the thick front end of the project; now it is all about execution and control.

'A whole is that which has beginning, middle and end.

Aristotle (384 BC   322 BC)

A number of aspects work well in the world of productive laziness – firstly ensuring that the project is conducted in a fun and enjoyable manner, and secondly being prepared to throw that newspaper down, leap off the comfy chair and deal with problems as and when they occur – but in a controlled and productive manner.

In addition, it is always good to spread a little love across your project team to engender good spirits and a confident air of potential success. Such love is a good thing but you do need to avoid the trap of being swamped with attention; you need to learn how to operate an open door policy but avoid getting dragged in to every little project detail.

All in a fun day's work

Taking it all a little less seriously can be good for your project health.

You have to laugh; well, I think you have to laugh.

'I love deadlines. I like the whooshing sound they make as they fly by.'

Douglas Adams, author of *The Hitchhiker's Guide to the Galaxy*

Without a little bit of fun in every project, the project world can be a dark and depressing place. Setting a professional but fun structure for your project can really be beneficial for the times when the problems start to rise up to challenge your plan of perfection. And problems will inevitably arise.

Over the years I have done many things to encourage team bonding, lighten the darker moments of project hell and diffuse difficult project-related situations. I have even accepted the full and complete blame for every problem, issue and challenge to a project in front of a room full of project team members, before walking outside and firing myself (in a loud voice, well, voices – one mine and one me pretending to be my boss). The net result was a diffused situation, where it had previously been extremely confrontational between teams and individuals.

Done well, this does not damage your status or authority. It can actually be a very positive act in people seeing you as a human being and not just a project manager, and thereafter wanting to share a smile and a laugh with you during the day.

It is just the same in that hotbed of confrontation, the home... Try looking at one of your children when they are in a really bad mood. Look them in the eye, with a serious face, point a finger at them and say 'Don't laugh! Don't you dare laugh! If you laugh you will go straight to the naughty stair!' I bet that at the very least you will get a smile out of them. My family finds that – even in the most stressed out, aggressive, emotional and 'in your face' moments – if you can make the opposition (and I use that term loosely) laugh, then the war is soon over.

It's hard to kill someone when you're laughing. Well, I guess that is true except for some of the more extreme psychopathic types.[19] ('No, I expect you to die, Mr Bond' ... cue maniacal laughter.)

APPLYING THE PRODUCTIVE LAZY APPROACH

Start with a smile and a joke

A project manager and her principal architect and chief analyst were having a lunchtime stroll along the beach, as you do, when they happened upon a small brass lamp lying on the sand. Eagerly, they grabbed the lamp and rubbed it and, of course, as in every fairytale, a giant genie appeared in a puff of magic smoke. 'I am the genie of the lamp,' he proclaimed, 'and I will grant you three wishes.' He paused, as if noting for the first time that there were in fact three people staring at him. 'As there are three of you, you will have to share the traditional three wishes. Each of you will be granted a wish each. Who's first?' he asked.

---

19. And you already know how to spot those people, don t you?

The ever-eager principal architect did not hesitate for a second. 'I wish that I was on a tropical island with sun, sand, clear blue water and palm trees, oh, and with a group of nubile girls delivering endless cocktails.'

'No problem,' said the genie, and with a quick flash and a puff of smoke the architect disappeared.

'Wow,' said the chief analyst. 'I wish I was in a fast and expensive sports car driving through the mountains to my magnificent villa overlooking the Mediterranean, where I will drink champagne and eat caviar.'

'Easy,' said the genie, and with another quick flash and puff of smoke the analyst disappeared as well.

'And what is your wish?' said the genie to the project manager.

'Simple,' she replied. 'I want those other two back at their desks by 1.30 prompt!'

Make fun part of your project

We all know about the team phases of 'forming – storming – norming – performing – mourning'[20] and if you don't there is plenty of information on the topic out there in search engine land.

---

20. The forming – storming – norming – performing model of group development was first proposed by Bruce Tuckman in 1965, who maintained that these phases are all necessary and inevitable in order for the team to grow, to face up to challenges, to tackle problems, to find solutions, to plan work and to deliver results. This model has become the basis for subsequent models of group development and team dynamics and a management theory frequently used to describe the behaviour of existing teams. Tuckman later added a fifth phase, adjourning, that involves completing the task and breaking up the team. Others call it the phase for mourning.

Now, I would suggest that to have a little bit of fun can really help calm the nerves during the storming phase when team conflict and competition can be high; it should be indoctrinated into the norming phase as the team develops their working rules and processes; and during the performing phase I am convinced of the value of fun in keeping the team at peak performance. Here are a few ideas.

A Canadian colleague and I used to put 'secret' fun messages in presentations that we gave. This allowed us to have a laugh or two, and in fact challenged us to put more and more difficult words and phrases into business presentations without anyone else spotting that something odd was going on. I extended this to a full project team once. No one knew that the others were in the game; everyone thought it was just them and me. It was very amusing. The meeting had a great feeling about it, everyone was happy and smiling. And, yes, it was very productive.

You can do things like 'It's Friday' the one day of the week when the team care share 'funnies' through email.[21] This is good because it limits (to a degree) such emails to one day of the week, and it should also make the team consider what is appropriate for general sharing rather than just sharing everything.

My current team all enjoy many happy moments, once a year, when we talk like a pirate on, honestly, 'Talk like a Pirate day'.[22] Check it out.

---

21. Check any policies that your company may have regarding non-business emails.

22. This is not a joke, it is a real 'international day' – visit www.talklikeapirate.com and have fun talking like a pirate, using email 'translators' to create pirate speech communication, and even slap on an eye patch and a parrot to get in to the mood. Just for the one day, you understand – any more than that and you are probably just odd.

And here is my favourite 'ice breaker'. Divide the group you have into small teams of four or five ideally; any more and it gets a little difficult. A flipchart or whiteboard is needed for each team (or at least a piece of flipchart paper). Get one person in each team to draw a large circle in the middle of each sheet and then draw a line out from that circle for each member of the team (so a team of four has four lines).

Now, giving them only about five minutes to do this, ask the teams to discuss amongst themselves and identify:

• Three things that they have in common.

• One thing that is unique to each of them.

Try to guide them away from really easy things like football, beer, work, shopping, etc. You want this to be informative and entertaining. Next they need to draw – pictures only, no words allowed – the things that they have discussed and identified. The things the team have in common should be drawn inside the circle, and the unique things should be drawn at the end of the lines; again, one unique thing per person. Allow ten minutes for them to do this.

When everyone is done, get the groups to remain standing and ask one person from each team to explain the team's results – for fun, see if the other teams can guess the nature of the unique things based on the drawings.

This process avoids the creeping death of introductions around the table and gets the group relaxed and knowing a little more about each other. It's surprising what you will find out about your colleagues in a very short time that you didn't know before, and I guarantee the results will be the topic of conversation at the next coffee break.

Practice safe fun

Obviously it has to be acceptable fun – I don't want to be 'PC' here but do be careful; think carefully about your team members. Does your idea of fun equal other people's fun? Also bear in mind there are times to have fun and times to be serious; you and your team must understand the parameters of this. And there may be members of the project team who just don't want to have fun, so make sure that they are not excluded or isolated from the rest of the team.

Make your fun smart fun

Now, when you have this whole 'work hard but have some fun' project underway the smart – and by that I, of course, mean productively lazy project managers – will sit back in their comfy chairs and let their project teams self-generate the fun working atmosphere.

Done properly, you will have set the acceptable parameters for fun in your project, both in content and in extent. You will also have engendered that spirit amongst your project team to the point where, one day, when you are the one on a low, they will come up and make you smile.

End with a laugh and a wave

A man in a hot air balloon was lost. He reduced altitude and spotted a woman below. He descended a little bit more and shouted 'Excuse me madam, can you help? I promised a friend I would meet him an hour ago, but I don't know where I am'.

The woman replied: 'You are in a hot air balloon hovering approximately thirty feet above alkali desert scrub habitat, 2.7 miles west of the Colorado River near one of the remnant populations and spawning grounds of the razorback sucker.'

'You must be a biologist,' said the balloonist.

'I am,' replied the woman. 'How did you know?'

'Well,' answered the balloonist, 'everything you told me is technically correct, but I have no idea what to make of your information, and the fact is that I'm still lost. Frankly, you've not been much help so far.'

The woman below responded with 'You must be a project manager.'

'I am,' answered the balloonist, 'but how did you know?'

'Well,' said the woman, 'you don't know where you are or where you're going. You have risen to where you are due to a large quantity of hot air. You made a promise to someone that you have no idea how to keep, and you expect me to solve your problem. The fact is that you are in exactly the same position you were in before we met, but somehow it's now my fault!'

Have fun on your projects.

('And, no, Mr Bond, I expect you to laugh.')

A PROJECT MANAGER'S TALE OF SELF-HUMILIATION

There was a time when I cared what others thought about me but that time has mostly passed; I still care a little, of course...

I think a significant turning point came a few years ago, not too many years ago come to think of it, when I was working on a global programme within my own company. The programme was simple in its concept – develop a standard project management methodology, train everybody in that methodology and then make sure that everyone used the methodology all of the time.

Parts one and two (develop and train) were not without their challenges but were achieved within twelve months, which was pretty good going. Part three proved to be the really difficult one. We met not with resistance as such, but more with apathy and a general mood of 'just smile politely and they will eventually leave us alone to carry on as we have always done'. Adoption rates were low and we were failing.

We had many (many) discussions, workshops, conference calls, brainstorming sessions and the like to try and work out what could be done to drive adoption that much faster. And all these ideas pretty much fell into two camps – the incentive category (or carrot) and the punishment category (stick).

One aspect of working on a global programme was that conference calls amongst the team were often held at unusually early or late times, and on one of these late long calls I had finally had enough. As the conversation went around and around the carrot and stick, stick and carrot, all carrot and no stick, all stick and no carrot options I suddenly stated 'What we actually need is the Giant Killer Carrot of Death'. Silence.

Laughter.

'Oh, we'd pay to see that,' was the general response and so, two weeks later – and having secured a suitable costume – I was outside my house having my photograph taken in a giant bright orange and green carrot outfit (I was very surprised when I contacted a large fancy dress hire company and requested a vegetable outfit. They listed a quite impressive list of options of both the vegetable and fruit variety). And so it came to pass that the Giant Killer Carrot of Death began his (do carrots have a sex?) reign of driving adoption in the methodology.

I really don't think that the whole root vegetable thing helped in any way with the future adoption levels of the methodology, but it certainly made the team laugh. It also gave them all a great introduction to many conversations, meetings and presentations after that (with the highest 'laugh' factor being the ones where they did this when I was also in the room): 'Have you seen Peter dressed as a carrot?'[23]

I like to think I made a few people's working day a little lighter. It was all in day's fun, that's for sure.[24]

---

23. Photographs can be obtained, one free with every 500 copies of *The Lazy Project Manager* purchased.

24. I was more than happy to 'take one for the team' in this way.

Breathing normally

The benefits of staying calm in a crisis.

You are on yet another flight, either to or from your latest project engagement, somewhere in the world. Maybe you have been lucky, maybe the flight is on time and you know your luggage is safely stored in the overhead locker, you are not seated in the middle seat between two sumo wrestlers with body odour and this flight does offer complimentary in-flight beverages.

You settle back in your seat and begin to drift into that 'yet another flight' snooze, vaguely aware that the air hostess is, for the thousandth time, explaining to you how to complete that complex conundrum of buckling and unbuckling your seat belt. You begin to disengage from the world around you...

But wait! The lady in the uniform, vainly talking to everyone but knowing no one is listening in return, is about to utter a supreme piece of wisdom. 'In the event of an emergency, an oxygen mask will drop in front of you from the panel above. Place the mask over your mouth and nose, straighten out the strap, and pull the strap to be sure it is tight on your face. After you are wearing it securely, a tug on the hose will start the oxygen flow. It makes sense to put your own mask on first, before helping others. Breathe normally.'

Breathe normally.

To begin with I used to think that this was the craziest thing possible. If I was ever on a flight where the oxygen masks were to drop down you can be sure that I would place the mask over my face, pull the strap as tight as possible, tug the hose until I felt the sweet taste of oxygen flowing. But the last thing I would be able to do would be breathe normally. I would breathe like it was my last moment on this earth (or air at this point, earth presumably being about to enter the equation in a rather nasty crashing, crushing, exploding sort of way). Breathe normally. Not a hope in hell!

But actually breathing normally is really, really good advice. Being calm, wasting less energy, wasting less oxygen, thinking clearly and considering the situation in a reasonable, objective manner is absolutely what is most likely to help you to survive.

In the project world when all around you are going crazy with panic (and that may well include the sponsor), breathing normally will allow you to consider the situation, assess the core issues, plan a response and carry out the actions with the minimum amount of effort and to the maximum effect.

APPLYING THE PRODUCTIVE LAZY APPROACH

Stay calm in a crisis

So, to begin with, you must stay calm in a crisis – really, this is most important.

The majority of potentially critical situations that you may well face in a project should have, in fact, already been considered as part of your risk planning and mitigation activity.[25] If you have done a complete and proper job at the start of the project (you remember, that point in time when even the productively lazy put in a solid day's work to get the project in the right shape to begin with) then you should have plans of action to hand for the majority of crises you are likely to face. Each eventuality should have been considered, reviewed, discussed, planned and have a conceptually proven response defined by yourself and your project team.

Plan for the crisis

If so, then for these situations you have at your fingertips a menu of actions that will mitigate or at least reduce the issues you are facing. No need to panic there, then.

That will still leave a small percentage of situations that you either did not consider as part of your risk strategy plan (this will be a learning exercise for you for future projects) or that have really blind-sided you because of their completely unexpected nature. Maybe the 'big red bus' that is so often joked about really has caused mayhem for you?

---

25. Risk management is activity directed towards the assessing, mitigating (to an acceptable level) and monitoring of risks. In some cases the acceptable risk may be near zero. Risks can come from accidents, natural causes and disasters as well as deliberate attacks from an adversary.

Breathe normally

Begin by counting to ten – seriously, try it. There is something in human nature that says that when a major issue has been identified, action is instantly required to resolve it. In reality, a short calming moment will allow a better chance of considering the issue in a more complete manner, and this in turn will result in a decision of action that is more likely to address both the issue at hand and any associated consequences. The last thing you want to do is put out one fire only to start another one somewhere else, one that could be worse than the first.

Equally, there is something else in human nature that can lead us to that 'rabbit in the headlights' state – frozen into complete inactivity by the oncoming crisis. With the project team looking to you to make a decision and set the required recovery plan into action, you do … nothing.

Breathe normally.

You need to be in control and you need to make the right decision, so look after yourself first – 'It makes sense to put your own mask on first, before helping others' – and once you are ready to consider your response to the problem then you should filter, filter, filter.

Filter, filter, filter

Identify the issue or issues and the source of those issues, and filter out those that either do not require you to resolve them or, indeed, are better resolved by others on the team. Nothing in the rule book says the project manager is the best person to deal with every issue, every crisis and every threat to the project's success. Quite the opposite is true, in fact. Don't try to be the project hero all of the time; it's not your job and the move from hero to zero comes damn fast!

Once you have filtered the issue or issues then take the next step which is to delegate, delegate, delegate. You have people in your project team for a good reason, so use them, use the breadth of their skills and knowledge to help you and the project overcome whatever is causing the problem.

Delegate, delegate, delegate

Remember that whilst a problem shared is a problem halved, a problem delegated is a problem not on your plate right now, leaving you free to get on with your real job, consider all implications of any recommended actions and oversee the project being steered back to safety. Hurrah!

Your one true job is to breathe normally.

Applying the productive lazy rule, I would personally aim for 80% of the issues being solved by others and maybe 20% of them being solved by you, or at least with you leading the resolution. You still don't have to do it all on your own.

So you have filtered (filtered, filtered) and you have delegated (delegated, delegated) and now what you need to do is to prioritise, prioritise, prioritise!

Prioritise, prioritise, prioritise

Even those issues that do end up on your plate may not need immediate and urgent action; maybe you have an issue coming at you but right now it is not showing signs of 'clear and present danger'. If so you have even more time to think and consider before you act.

Deal with the ones that you have to and monitor the others that you don't have to deal with right now. For those that can wait a little, maybe you can consider options of action that are open to you and the team ready for the future. Gather insight from your team members and any other source of knowledge that you can reach out to, and continue to do that single most important thing.

Breathe normally.

A PROJECT MANAGER'S TALE OF ENDURING THE PERFECT STORM

At the height of a particular project, and working with a particularly demanding team of people, the project I was managing some years ago hit a problem. Now the problem was, initially, undefined, the cause unknown, but the effects were quite worrying.

Let me paint the picture a little more. There was a deadline, a quite aggressive deadline, and there was the steering committee, a quite aggressive steering committee. There was also a project sponsor, of course, an extremely demanding, loud, opinionated, driven individual who I was convinced never actually wanted to see this particular project succeed (quite an unusual project sponsorship position but one which I was sure this person had taken).

Anyway, the deadline loomed towards us on the project team and the technical challenges seemed never-ending; as quickly as one was resolved another (if not more than one) seemed to take its place. The working days got longer and the toll of all this pressure began to cause serious stress faults in the project team; their ability to work together became fragile, shall we say. The slightest thing had people at my desk or on the phone complaining.

In the midst of all this fractious harmony we hit the problem. I won't go into the details of the actual problem itself, it was technical and complicated to understand – but not complicated to resolve, it turned out.

Now, if the team had been at full efficiency and working as one, I am sure we would have spotted the cause earlier and resolved the issue quickly and quietly. As it was, we didn't do either of them. The cause went unresolved and the effects seemed to spiral ever onwards, on towards being out of control completely. Rapid response meetings were convened, but all the team seemed to do was argue and point fingers of blame at each other as well as at any and every other part of the organisation.

A lot of different problem-solving techniques were attempted, and no doubt some real out of the box, blue sky thinking was applied, but without success. Everybody was trying to resolve this issue. Some even headed to the pub to try and find a cure there; such dedication should be admired.

Anyway, the result? Well, the result was a whole bunch of 'headless chickens' running around the place and each and every one of them stopped doing their day job. This resulted in further delays threatening the project, and put ever-increasing pressure on the poor project manager (me) who had to provide updates to the steering committee and project sponsor. A less than relaxing experience.

Just when I really thought it was all going to implode I had one of those 'eureka' moments. I can't say it was planned and I can't say it was done in a positive or creative spirit. It was, if I am completely honest, done in a moment when I just lost my temper. I ordered various parts of my project team off to various parts of the company offices to 'go and do their jobs and get us back on track'. Inadvertently I gave a number of people the authority to stop worrying about 'the problem' and to concentrate once more on their scheduled tasks. In addition to this, and once again I can claim no real skill in orchestrating it, I was left with one fairly junior technical guy and, for the want of anything else to do, told him to head off to the IT department and find someone who could help think this problem through.

And what did I do? Well, I was the one who went to the pub. I admit it, I just needed to escape the pressure and think. I had fallen in to the trap of becoming subjective in all the chaos and panic, and I know now I should have remained above everything and objective in my view.

What happened then were three things.

Firstly, I had a very nice steak pie, chips and peas with a pint of beer. Secondly, the junior technical guy just happened to talk to the right person – in fact, the right person was a combination of the right person inside the company and, purely by chance at that point, the right person visiting from another part of the company. And thirdly, the issue was initially worked around and later resolved through some third-party intervention.

I was lucky, the crisis passed and the project staggered on for a while and eventually delivered; later than expected but, nevertheless, it did deliver.

It did teach me an important lesson. Filter what you should deal with, delegate everything you can, prioritise what is left and then focus on what is important. In this case I did none of these things and was lucky to get the result I did.

A lot of 'lurve' in the room

It's not about you, no, really it isn't.

It's a team thing!

Well, that's a truth, but there are many and varied ways of working with teams, leading teams, managing teams and getting the very best out of teams. People, as well you know, are immensely complicated things.

Your approach may well vary depending upon the nature of project management in the organisation in which you are working. Is this a one-off or are you likely to have some of the team members on your next project? Is the project driven for the greater good of all or is this a business change critical project where people are expendable? It's a jungle out there sometimes and only you and your sponsor will know the needs of your projects. Some projects will allow for people development and some will not.

You can read and learn from many sources on the means of assessing team members, characterising them, identifying optimum working partnerships and working styles, and generally getting the best out of the team as a whole. Equally you can read about driving teams to the very 'edge of chaos' where a team can actually deliver magnificent productivity, but with a limited and potentially fatal shelf life for those in the team.

So many choices but, as a general rule, consider this: a little love goes a long way and a lot of love goes much further. Consider your team, care for your team, love your team but don't marry them. Treat them like a lover; flirt with them, tease them, treat them, (lie to them if you really have to) but never, ever promise them that the relationship is forever. It isn't! It is just for the lifetime of the project – remember that.

APPLYING THE PRODUCTIVE LAZY APPROACH

Make your project attractive

If you can get people wanting to work with you and wanting to join your project then that offers a huge benefit straight from day one. You may not want all of them on your team and you may want some people who haven't lined up begging to join the party, but at least you know that either you are popular to work with and/or the project you are heading up is seen as an exciting one with career potential for would-be team members.

People will seek your project out for a number of reasons:

* You (your sheer charisma, track record of success, reputation for team support or development, etc).

* Recommendation from others (based on the above list).

* The project (high profile, new and exciting, groundbreaking, business critical, etc).

* The project opportunity (more senior project role, multi-company, multi-country, global, etc).

All good things, I'm sure you would agree.

* Nothing better available.

A bad thing without a doubt. Well, possibly, but if this is a resource you could really do with then it may work, or you just have to make it work. Being popular is great, but be cautious and understand the motives that drive people towards you.

Get the best team that you can

A great old maxim for project teams is 'Something old, something new, something borrowed, something blue'.[26] Traditionally linked to the bride's outfit at weddings, it can mean, for a project, someone with experience (old), someone with enthusiasm (new), someone brought in to the team from outside the project/department, etc. who brings an objective viewpoint (borrowed), and someone not afraid to speak their minds and drive the team hard (blue – as in a little bit of swearing to make the point count).

Alternatively, you may be given a project team with little or no choice. At the very least try and get a known and skilled 'number two' to work with you, whether that is a support project manager, administrator, project office coordinator, whatever.

A 'good' project team is not just about the right skills but also about the right levels of enthusiasm and energy.

26. The custom is based on an English poem: something old, something new, something borrowed, something blue and a silver sixpence in her shoe. The custom is that if the bride carries all four items on her wedding day, she will have a happy marriage. Each verse refers to a good luck item:

Something old – continuity with the bride's family and the past.

Something new – optimism and hope for the bride's new life ahead.

Something borrowed – an item from a happily married friend or family member, whose good fortune in marriage is supposed to carry over to the new bride.

Something blue – before the late nineteenth century, blue was a popular colour for wedding dresses.

Feed the feel-good factor

Once you have your team you need to help them bond quickly, work together productively (so you can be lazy and chill out in the comfy chair), and resolve problems in a calm way whilst communicating to each other, and you, in a simple and effective manner. Simple really.

Your team, assuming that you have all your roles fulfilled, will need the following in order to be fully effective:

- Clarity of the goals of the project.

- Belief in those goals.

- Trust in you and their project colleagues.

- Rules and processes for working.

- Respect for each other.

I would also add the ability and freedom to openly challenge anyone and anything, as long as it is done in a constructive and non-confrontational way.

With all this in place then the feel-good factor can thrive. You just have to feed it with your support and enthusiasm. (A reasonable budget for social activities doesn't do any harm either.)

Consider: is it nature or nurture?

It's a very lucky project manager who assumes control of a project and a project team and finds that they work at optimum performance from day one (all the way through to day 'end'). No, the reality is that you will need to do some work to help make this happen.

Going back to the list above:

* Clarity of the goals of the project – it is your job to explain this clearly.

* Belief in those goals – it is your job to ensure that you believe that they believe (if even you don't believe then there is no hope), and if they don't believe to convert them.

* Trust in you and their project colleagues – this can only be achieved through experience, proving that trust is there day by day.

* Rules and processes for working – again this is up to you to present, educate, publish, promote and enforce.

* Respect for each other – you must manage this; respect is inherent in human nature but you do need to keep a close eye on it and deal with any instances where a lack of respect is identified.

* Freedom to be open in their views – encourage this from day one, at project meetings, one-to-ones, team social events, audits and reviews and, at the end of projects, retrospectives. It is not just about being open to listening to people but also about following up on suggestions and comments.

Spot the carers

A lot of the things above you need to do as the project manager, but mostly at the start of the project. Along the way you could identify project team members who are 'carers' or 'nurturers', and use them; it will help you and it will make them feel good.

These people are closest to the Belbin[27] team role of Teamworker. They are good listeners and diplomats, talented at smoothing over conflicts and helping parties understand each other without becoming confrontational. The beneficial effect of a Teamworker is often not noticed until this person is absent, when the team begins to argue and small but important things cease to happen. These are the people who will naturally help others, quickly and without fuss, and will present issues to you that are not technical or operational but of a more personal nature.

Use all of your project team's skills and talents. Just because you recruited team member A because of their known skill at technology X, does not mean that they cannot utilise their personnel skill of Y (where Y could well be the skill of organising project social events, keeping tracking of team members' birthdays, and being aware of any personal issues, etc).

27. The Belbin Team Role Inventory assesses how an individual behaves in a team environment. It is therefore a behavioural tool, subject to change, and not a psychometric instrument. The assessment includes 360-degree feedback from observers as well as the individual s own evaluation of their behaviour, and contrasts how they see their behaviour with how their colleagues do. The Belbin Inventory scores people on how strongly they express traits from nine different team roles. An individual may, and often does, exhibit strong tendencies towards multiple roles.

There is a lot of 'science' out there to help you analyse your project team members if you wish – as already mentioned, there's Belbin, and there is also Myers-Briggs,[28] for example. But equally you can learn a lot by just watching your team members working, in teams, alone, at meetings and so on. And in talking to them – don't forget that it is good to talk (and not just about project matters, either).

Analyse the love required

As with communication, covered earlier, you should 'customise' the love you give to each recipient. Everyone wants something different. Find out what they want and provide it – as long as it is earned. Do it privately or publicly as is warranted, or indeed required by the recipient, and do try and avoid the 'Oscar speech' syndrome[29] where you thank everyone and their mother and their mother's pet poodle for this wonderful, wonderful project and all the wonderful support you have received and how you will miss them all so terribly. Keep it real!

28. The Myers-Briggs typology model regards personality type as similar to left or right handedness: individuals are either born with, or develop, certain preferred ways of thinking and acting. The MBTI sorts some of these psychological differences into four opposite pairs, or 'dichotomies', with a resulting sixteen possible psychological types. None of these types is 'better' or 'worse'. The different types are extroversion, sensing, thinking, judging and then introversion, intuition, feeling and perceiving.

29. Greer Garson is credited with having given the longest acceptance speech in the history of the Academy Awards. The next year, speech length was capped. Legend tells of her oration being as long as twenty minutes, but in actual fact it was only about seven minutes.

A PROJECT MANAGER'S TALE OF INAPPROPRIATE LOVE

I was working on a project, not as the project manager this time but in a quality support role that required my involvement in a part-time manner over a period of months. During that time I was invited, as a matter of politeness I am sure, to a number of team social events.

The project had passed through a pilot phase and had been duly proven and was ready for deployment at a number of locations across the UK, France and Germany. This roll out was managed by a team of people who had assisted in the pilot project and who had now graduated to ownership and management of the project proper. As a risk precaution, I was there to review key documents and milestones and generally make sure the project was in good health and on track.

Now, this team liked to party. They travelled around the countries, stayed in nice hotels, ate well on expenses (and it must be admitted, drank well on expenses too), as well as having a team-building budget that was quite impressive. The project manager was a gregarious guy who loved all things 'outdoors' and as a result the social events, which began with a few beers and a meal, progressed quickly through bowling and go-karting ever upwards until about twelve months into the project he came up with a biggie.

We were all on location number four, which was in the process of going live, and the project manager and most of the team were feeling very pleased with themselves. Time to party!

I had begun to notice that one member of the team, the guy who was in charge of preparing each location for deployment, was beginning to get a little less organised. The preparation work was being rushed, it seemed, and errors were being made that impacted the deployment work. The model was that he would spend a week on site ahead of the rest of the team to complete this preparation work, be joined by the full team whilst they deployed (this took four weeks in total) but leave them a week early in order to move on and prepare the next location.

Things came to a head during the time the full team was at the fourth location. Firstly, the mistakes that had been made in preparation this time caused a lot of problems and the team was less than happy about it. Fingers were angrily pointed at 'Mr. Preparation'. Secondly, the project manager decided to run a team-building experience at the weekend – lots of fresh air, cold rivers, open fields, tall trees and bridge building with cocktail sticks and drink cans (or something like that). I happened to be with the team for one of my regular reviews.

Suddenly Mr. P went absent without leave – he just disappeared. It took two days to get confirmation that he had just checked out of the hotel, jumped into his car and headed home.

Since I was only required on site for two days, and had not been invited to the weekend experience of a lifetime, I volunteered to go and call on Mr. P when I got back and see if I could find out what the problem was. And so I did.

It turned out that our Mr. P was the only one who was married out of all the people on the project team. The rest of the team were single or content not to spend so much time around their respective partners. In addition, Mr. P had no taste for the great outdoors or partying in general and actually preferred a much quieter life. And, thirdly, he felt that he had never received any praise for his work. He was alone on site doing the preparatory work, which had no glory attached to it, and he left the site before the location went live and therefore missed the time when everyone was thanked for all their hard work.

Mr. P was a good guy, a valuable asset to the team, good at his job. But, unconsidered and unknown by the rest of his team and his project manager, he had volunteered for this role for the very reason that he could avoid some of the partying and excesses of the rest of the team. He was so detached from the decision-making process that he had no say on the roll-out schedule and as a result ended up with very little time to be at home. The rest of the team loved the fact that they were never at home and lived for 90% of the time at the company's expense. Lastly, Mr P's tastes were never considered when the social events were planned. To begin with he joined in to be part of the team but later on he joined in because he had to.

I can't say I was close enough or clever enough to have spotted this any earlier, but it was a good lesson that I learned from the sideline. Consider what love each of your team members needs. In this case even the most basic of information about one team member was not recognised by the rest.

Was there a happy ending? Well, initially Mr P went back and trained another team member in his preparation duties with a plan to rotate the team roles a little, but this lasted less than six months. He eventually elected to take another job, within the same company but close to home. Where he was happy.

The lights are on (but no one's at home)

Being accessible – but in a controlled way.

I'm all for being there for people, honest I am. It's just that people take advantage of it if I am.

So, for the productive lazy project manager I would suggest that it is perfectly acceptable for the lights to be on and for no one to be at home – not all of the time, obviously, and at critical times access and visibility are all too important. But for the rest of the time, why not let the whole of the team work a few things out for themselves, take some degree of responsibility and decision-making, and generally get on with the tasks at hand?

Being there when you are really needed and being there all the time are very different things indeed.

Being reachable in a controlled manner, and within an acceptable timeframe, to answer appropriate questions (and not stupid ones) is equally important. The last thing you want is a long line of people queuing up at your desk waiting to ask advice, your phone flashing with an ever-increasing number of messages, while all the time your in-box is reaching capacity with demands for your attention.

This can lead to the 'lights on all the time' syndrome, a very dangerous condition:

'What should I do now?'

'Breathe,' you might reply.

'In or out?'

You have so many other more useful things that you could be doing, like reading a good book in the comfy chair, for example.

APPLYING THE PRODUCTIVE LAZY APPROACH

Avoid the swamp

This is linked in so many ways to the communication topic already covered. If you create a communication plan that guarantees to swamp you from day one, what is the benefit, either to you or to the project? None.

The plan should ensure that you are not seen as the oracle in all matters, nor that you are the bottleneck for a constructive information flow within the project team. Most projects develop communication plans in a certain way: that is, as a plan which is the documented strategy for getting the right information to the right people at the right time. We all know that each stakeholder has different requirements for information and so the plan defines what, how and how often communications should be made. What project managers rarely do is consider and map all communication flows, official, unofficial, developmental or complete, and do a load analysis across the project structure of these communication flows. If they did they would spot bottlenecks much earlier on than they normally do; usually they are only identified when one part of the communication chain starts complaining about the workload.

Consider the open door policy

The open door policy has become a real management cliché. 'Of course,' a manager pronounces in a firm voice, 'my door is always open to you all, day or night; I'm really there for you.'

Empowerment in this way has become more an entitlement for the project team than a project manager's choice; they just expect you to be there when they want you to be (and not even when they need you to be there, either). An open door policy can easily transform a project manager's role from that of an authority, and managing, figure to that of a subservient accommodator with little chance for exercising control on those who demand access.

Be a good manager

The best manager is probably the one who reads the paper or MSN every morning, has time enough to say 'hi' at the coffee machine, and isn't always running flat out because they are 'late for an important meeting'. By that I mean that a good (an obviously productively lazy) manager has everything running smoothly enough so that they have time to read the paper or MSN and so on. These are managers who have to be confident in their position and capabilities.

Good managers will have time for their project team, and being people who have everything running smoothly, will allow that to happen. Good managers do not have to be on hand twenty-four hours a day, seven days a week. They do not have to have the answer to every question nor do they have to be the conduit to the answer to every question.

There is a whole project team out there, so go and talk to some of them; they will probably have a much better answer to hand anyway.

Think about number one

You honestly want the best for yourself as well as for the project; I understand that, so give yourself that chance. Have you ever met a project manager who has put themselves down as a project risk? 'Yeah, well I am just too nice, can't say no, can't turn someone away, love to chat' – likelihood 80%, impact 100%, mitigate now!

But hopefully, by now, you also want to apply the productive lazy approach so consider this: let the team deal with 80% of the communication, 80% of the questions, 80% of the issues, and let the 20% come through you for consideration and guidance. You don't even have to 'solve' that 20%; I would further suggest that only 20% of this 20% are likely to be answered by you in an adequate manner. There are always others who can give better advice.

Think about the rest

OK, you have dealt with the 'thinking about number one' thing, now what about your team? Well, by dealing with number one you will have already done the team a huge favour. You will be accessible when you need to be accessible. The lights will go on as and when they are really needed – it is a kind of 'green' project management policy.

The worst thing that can happen is that just at the moment when there is a 'clear and present' need for someone to speak to you, whether that be on a project or on a personal matter, you are too tied up with a whole pile of nothing to even give them the time of day. Remember the whole 'respect' and 'reputation for team support' team thing I mentioned earlier? Well, this is a major contributor to that.

Analyse and reduce

And this is not a one-off action; you need to keep on top of this as well. Projects change, communications develop and roles flux. Do a quick analysis of what information and queries flow through you, and how, and regularly reassess. Can others deal with some of this? What are the important components that you should be involved in? Are there too many questions and communications from certain sources? And so on.

Make sure that everyone knows that the lights will go on and when and how they can turn that light on fast if they really need to.

A PROJECT MANAGER'S TALE ABOUT THE IMPORTANCE OF POSITION

This one is not my own tale; it is the story of a friend of mine, a friend who is, of course, a project manager. A project manager I know to be very good at team building, a real 'people' person.

Picture a new project with a new project office. Apparently the company my friend was working for had reserved some brand new office space in a building that they were going to move other departments to in the coming months. In the meantime the project team could take over one floor.

Now, I have been in many project offices over the years, ranging from a single desk to a temporary office unit (grey boxes that get lifted in to place by a crane and officially described as 'relocatable and modular accommodation', apparently). But, by all accounts, this new building that my friend moved into with his project team was superb. He chose a nice new desk by a window and with a view facing the doors so that he could see all that went on, people coming and going, working (or not working, I guess), and so on. And so life was good and thus did the project move forwards in a pleasing way.

The only feature that was lacking was a decent coffee machine. They had a temporary one to begin with but the team waited with baited breath for the new, top of the range, super-dooper, hot beverage dispenser.

It arrived one weekday morning, wheeled in on a trolley. My friend was elsewhere at the time on important project business. When he arrived back in the project office he was somewhat surprised to see that his desk now had a new neighbour. A coffee machine.

'Hey, grab a coffee, its great,' was the general cry from the project team. I am sure that that is what he did, before walking the two feet back to his desk. The project office was full now and so it was too late to move. Oh, well, a great project office with a great coffee machine was not something to make too much fuss about. And then things went downhill.

Day 1:   People started saying 'hello' each time they lined up for a coffee at the machine by his desk.

Day 2:   People started conversations as they waited for their 'freshly brewed' cup of java by his desk.

Day 3:   People started sitting on his desk whilst they waited for coffee, said 'hello', engaged in conversation and were generally sociable.

Day 4:   People asked him where the spare coffee cups were and what 'error 54g' was.

Day 5:   People asked him what the telephone number for the coffee repairman was so that they could report 'error 54g' and get the coffee machine fixed.

Day 10:   People started using the phone on his desk whilst waiting for a coffee, etc.

Day 15:   The project manager left the building.

In actual fact he did move desks; he managed to secure a small space across the landing from the main project office. It wasn't ideal as he was now removed from the project team but, on balance, it was better than the alternative.

It doesn't matter that you want to run an open door policy in order to be as accessible to everyone; if you want to get on with your job you do need some space. To be right at the centre of everything all of the time is not conducive to being a good project manager. It was the coffee machine or the project manager, and the team made it clear that the coffee machine won hands down!

Then thick again at the far end

Time for one last effort, to make life easier in the future.

The Lazy Project Manager's theory of projects, from a productive laziness aspect: 'All projects are thick at one end, much, much thinner in the middle and then thick again at the far end.'

'The world is round and the place which may seem like the end may also be only the beginning.

Ivy Baker Priest

Now is not the time to declare the project a success and rush off for a Bloody Mary[30] at the bar.

No, now is the time that you can apply a small and final amount of effort but gain enormous amounts of knowledge so that future projects are likely to be even more successful and potentially take even less effort. And less effort, we know, means so much more time in the comfy chair, being lazy but in a productive way.

---

30. I am not advocating that project managers need to drink alcohol. An alternative recipe to a Bloody Mary (my favourite cocktail) is a Virgin Mary: 125 ml tomato juice, one teaspoon Worcestershire sauce, one dash lemon juice, two drops Tabasco sauce, pepper and salt. Stir with ice in a large wine glass. Garnish with a wedge of lime.

The missing link

Either you have been missing something, or nothing has really
been going on.

'As we know, there are
known knowns. There are
things we know we know.
We also know there are
known unknowns. That is
to say we know there are
some things we do not
know. But there are also
unknown unknowns.
The ones we don t know
we don t know.

Donald Rumsfeld
(12 February, 2002, US Department
of Defense news briefing).

That is one crazy set of words
but actually there is a lot of
sense in the whole thing. Here
you are at the end of the
project. It has been a success
or, at the very least, has not
been a complete failure, and
you are about to head off to
the next project. But wait,
do you really honestly know
everything? Do you know
what you don't know? Well
of course you don't, you can't
possibly. So don't fool yourself
that you do!

So what do you do about it?
Well, what you do about it is do something about it – now is the time to
conduct a retrospective of your project, a review, a considered and open
activity that will allow you the opportunity to learn what it is you don't
yet know.

Just as at the start of the project – remember, 'a shiny brand new project … at a point in time that is full of peace and love and general well-being between all parties involved' – well, the end of the project is a special time as well. It is a time when project team members are far more likely to talk to you openly, equally and honestly. Therefore it is a time you should really focus some effort on in order to learn how to be more effective (and even more productively lazy) next time around.

APPLYING THE PRODUCTIVE LAZY APPROACH

Finish what you started

As the Mastermind[31] question master says, 'I've started and so I'll finish', and you should make sure that you do the same. Finish the project in a correct and complete manner. Avoid all of those normal pressures and temptations to head off on the next juicy project that is calling you. Make the very most of this second opportunity of peace, love and harmony (hopefully) and learn everything that you can learn. It will be worth it, I guarantee.

Know what you know

Start with yourself. What do you 'know' about the project? Well, a whole load of stuff that's for sure, but focus less on what you already knew at the start of the project and think more about what you have learned during the project. Much of what happened will have been processed, dealt with, handled through the re-application of past experience or knowledge, but some will not have been. You learn through each project, so consider what it is that you learned this time.

---

31. Mastermind is a British quiz show, well-known for its challenging questions, intimidating setting and air of seriousness. The basic format of Mastermind has never changed – four contestants face two rounds, one on a specialised subject of the contestant s choice, the other a general knowledge round.

Now you know what you know and probably also know what you don't know – gaps in your experience on the project, questions you can ask your team.

Find out what you don t know

Now focus on the unknown unknowns.

The ideal way to do this is to conduct a full retrospective; if you can't do this, then at least gather input from key members of your project team. One of the best reference books for this is *Project Retrospectives* by Norman L. Kerth (see References). I love the prime directive that Kerth governs his retrospectives by: 'Regardless of what we discover, we must understand and truly believe that everyone did the best job he or she could, given what was known at the time, his or her skills and abilities, the resources available, and the situation at hand.'

There are treasures out there, no single person knows all there is to know about the project and certainly not you, the project manager (you don't honestly think your team told everything that went on, do you?).

So go mining, there are nuggets of gold in 'lessons learned' or at least lessons to be learned if only you pay attention. At least one of your project team will tell you something that will aid you in the future and let you be a little more productively lazy. And the best way to make this happen is to plan for it to happen, right back at the thick front end of the project, back at the very beginning.

Ask what you now need to know

As part of this retrospective process make sure that you also take the opportunity to ask questions that you want answering. Remember? The things that you know you don't know, the gaps in your experience on the project, the questions you should ask your team.

Complete your knowledge by having an open and honest dialogue with the team. What you don't know may surprise them, and they will, no doubt, be pleased that they were able to help out during the project.

Learn the lessons to be learned

OK, now let's sum all this up. Carefully and slowly.

* You know what you know.

* You also know what you don't know – and have received answers to the gaps in your knowledge, hopefully.

* You now know what you didn't know you knew, through feedback from the team and other sources.

* And, through the retrospective, you at least know a little more about what you didn't know that you didn't know – if the team have been very open with you.

Simple, isn't it?

Tell others what you now know

Finally, don't just sit on that knowledge. Share it out amongst everyone who could benefit from it. Lessons learned should be lessons shared, so don't be mean, share it out!

Time for one last grid,[32] the grid of self-development logic.

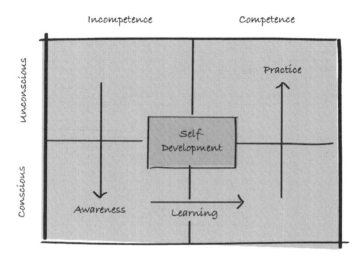

All the above can be summarised in this diagram. To move from unconscious incompetence to conscious incompetence, not knowing what you don't know and just not caring, you need awareness – and the retrospective can aid this awareness.

---

32. I am sure that you noticed my affection for all things grid-like. We all know that a picture is supposed to paint a thousand words, or something like that, and a picture is easier to remember. Therefore, logically, a simple picture is that much easier to remember when you need to.

To move from conscious incompetence to conscious competence, knowing what you don't know but caring about that fact – again the retrospective can help, along with a learning plan based on the outputs.

And to move from conscious competence to unconscious competence – well, that just requires a lot of practice, so get to it!

A PROJECT MANAGER'S TALE OF ESCAPE WITHOUT CAUSE

One final story, and again, I am the project manager in question, much to my shame.

For the most part I have really enjoyed all of my projects. That is not to say that there haven't been challenges over the years; high points and low points, moments when I felt that I had had enough but equally good moments that I didn't want to end. This tale, however, is of a project within a manufacturing company that had a lot more low points than high ones.

The project was 'challenging' (and seemed close to impossible at times), the steering committee were 'difficult' (to say the least), the project team were 'mixed' in their interest and capability (to put it mildly), and I was a long way from home. The entire experience really tested me as a project manager pretty much from day one, but I felt that I had acquitted myself in a good way. In a good way until the very end of the project, that is.

So, to quickly move to the point of this story, the project reached a conclusion. The deliverables were delivered and the company reluctantly agreed to signing off the project. The job was done. Except it wasn't.

I had had quite a hellish experience over the months and just wanted it all to come to an end. And so, when that final steering committee meeting was done and the minutes signed off, I have to admit that I almost ran to my car, jumped in and tore out of the car park, deliriously happy. The motorway home called to me and, with some rock music blaring out of the speakers[33], I decided to write this one off to history and never return again. I was one happy project manager.

Then I was asked to go back to a post-project review!

My heart sank and I began to make up 101 reasons why I was too busy, too sick, too mentally incompetent, too 'about to go on a spontaneous holiday' and too 'I just don't want to go back' in order to, well, avoid going back.

I didn't go back. Someone else did. And so that was that.

Except it wasn't. My inquisitiveness eventually got the better of me and I sat down with the other project manager, sometime after the review, and discovered many things that I had never known about my own project. I discovered (obviously through this other project manager) that the company had had a very bad experience in a similar previous project and, as a result, they were nervous about this project, very nervous indeed. I discovered that the project had been strongly championed by one of the steering members despite a lot of resistance from others in the business and that a lot – this person's reputation and possibly career, for example – depended upon a successful outcome. I discovered that two people on the project team had,

---

33. It was Black Sabbath, 'Sabotage', if I remember rightly (and if you care at all), a classic band and album that I still enjoy these days. Now along with Jenny, my daughter, who has inherited much of her father s wisdom.

shall we say, personal 'issues' during the early part of the project and this led to some residual tension between them. I discovered that there was felt to be a black hole in one particular business area where the purpose and benefit, the justification, of the project was never explained. I discovered that they thought that I was a very strong and competent project manager, but one who didn't perhaps focus enough on the human side of the project.

And I personally discovered, and I did not have to be told this by my project management colleague, that I had missed a great deal by leaving the project before its final conclusion. I personally discovered that I should have stayed for the full and proper closure. I would have learned so much.

Quick tips to productive lazy heaven

I'll take one of those, but do you have it in a smaller size please?

What did I miss?

If you were amongst those who didn't cheat and read conscientiously through all the chapters then you didn't miss anything; you can go straight to productive heaven with my blessing.

But if you did cheat then, hey, you missed a lot!

You missed something really interesting about eating dinosaurs, wearing ermine cloaks and how to spot a psychopathic woman at a funeral. We discovered the use for a creep'o'meter, learned much more about Swedish sex in the snow, and why you should never go ballooning. We avoided a big red bus, learned how to deliver a good Oscar acceptance speech, and appreciated why it is important for your team that you read the newspaper each morning. Oh, and we discovered a little something about mining for gold. We may also have briefly mentioned project management.

But don't worry, it wasn't all that important. Don't feel you have to go all the way back just to catch up.

Take me to productive heaven now

So I guess the question is this: in order to learn to become productively lazy, with all the application of the science of laziness, the 80/20 rule, the lazy to smart ratio, and all that, can you, the reader, apply the lazy rule to the lazy learning curve in an even more lazy way and basically get up the lazy learning curve in a faster way?[34]

Put it this way, out of everything I have mentioned in this book so far, does the very principle that is the essence behind the theory mean that only 20% of what has been covered in the previous pages is really, really critical in adapting your project management work style in order to achieve the productive lazy life? Can you sweat it a whole lot less in order to join me in the comfy chair?

An interesting theory. Shall we test it?

---

34. There is 'Pareto' science behind this, by the way, are you ready? OK, mathematically, where something is shared among a sufficiently large set of participants, there will always be a number k between 50 and 100 such that k% is taken by (100 – k)% of the participants; however, k may vary from 50 in the case of equal distribution (e.g. exactly 50% of the people take 50% of the resources) to nearly 100 in the case of a tiny number of participants taking almost all of the resources. There is nothing special about the number 80, but many systems will have k somewhere around this region of intermediate imbalance in distribution. This is a special case of the wider phenomenon of Pareto distributions. If the parameters in the Pareto distribution are suitably chosen, then one would have not only 80% of effects coming from 20% of causes, but also 80% of that top 80% of effects coming from 20% of that top 20% of causes, and so on (80% of 80% is 64%; 20% of 20% is 4%, so this implies a '64-4 law').

Well, you will have arrived here in one of two ways. Directly, from the 'Can I cheat?' chapter – in which case you are most likely to be impatiently lazy with a desire for rapid productiveness, and that will be either a good thing or a foolhardy thing; only you and your mother can be the judge of that. Alternatively, you have progressed honestly and carefully through all the intervening chapters to arrive here in both a calm and fully prepared state. And that can only be a good thing; no need to involve your mother on this one.

Whichever, the following should be useful to you in several ways: for short-cutting the whole process and proving to yourself that you are already lazy and productive, as reference material for future application of the theory of productive laziness or possibly as proof to yourself that you need to go back and read all the chapters between 'Can I Cheat?' and this one since you don't have a clue what the following material is all about.

Let's see if it works. Ready?

OK, well, cutting out 80% of the content of the learning points from the preceding chapters and focusing on the remaining 20% gives something like this:

1. A project: thick at one end, thin in the middle, then thick again at the other end, absolutely not like a dinosaur but like a project.

2. A project: thick at the start or initiation; no time for rest right now, work hard and rest later.

3. It is important for you to stay ahead of the game:

    a. Start as you mean to go on and be confident, as this does breed success.

    b. Dress smartly and get the upper hand as soon as you can; stay on that moral high ground for as long as you can and always be prepared.

    c. Anticipate everything you can and keep your eye on the end game so that you can drive the project in a direct manner towards conclusion and success.

4. You need to manage your sponsor:

    a. So ask them what they expect from you and the project, but do make sure you manage the first meeting and use the right questions and have an open discussion with them.

    b. Apply the power grid to help you understand your sponsor better and appreciate the types of power that they may have.

    c. Also appreciate that understanding what is in it for your sponsor will aid your ability to work with them.

5. And you need to manage the project creep:

    a. Creep is inevitable but there is nothing wrong with measuring the potential creepiness of the project team in order to be better prepared.

    b. Manage the change process on your project and use the process immediately as a showcase and education for your team.

c. If you can't use the suggestion or request then park it in the parking lot – but don't forget it and thank contributors for their ideas, always.

6. You must avoid a communication breakdown at all costs:

   a. You must communicate as others need you to communicate, understand how communication works and be honest and be open in your communication.

   b. Effective but minimal communication is better than ineffective and overwhelming communication.

   c. Appreciate that modern communication is both a benefit and a hindrance; communicate the communication plan to everyone and stress that reporting is not communicating.

7. A project: thin in the middle – do it right and this is where you get to rest, a lot; do it wrong, and you will be busy all day, every day.

8. Have fun, it's all in a day's work and it will help the project along nicely:

   a. So start with a smile and a joke and appreciate that you have to laugh to make fun part of your project.

   b. But always practice safe fun, and don't offend anyone.

   c. If you are smart with your people then fun will be an inherent part of your project and you won't have to do very much at all; just make sure that you end with a laugh and a wave.

9. Breathe normally at all times:

   a. Stay calm in a crisis, and one way to do this is to get the planning right and not panic but just breathe normally when you do hit a problem.

   b. Always filter, filter, filter then delegate, delegate, delegate and finally prioritise, prioritise, prioritise each and every problem that comes your way.

   c. Breathe normally at all times in order to make the right decisions to keep the project on track.

10. Make sure that there is lot of 'lurve' in the room:

    a. First, do the groundwork and make your project attractive to others.

    b. Then get the best team that you can and feed the feel-good factor so that the team really feels that they are appreciated, and in the right way.

    c. Consider whether it's nature or nurture that will make the feel-good factor thrive in this project; help yourself by spotting the carers you may have on the team and make sure that you analyse the love that each team member requires.

11. It is OK for the lights to be on and no one at home, within reason:

    a. So avoid swamping yourself with communication and demands for your time.

    b. Have an open door policy, but also be a good manager and control the open door access.

c. Think about number one – you – for the greater good of the project team and keep analysing and reducing, where you need to, your involvement. Others may have better solutions or answers.

12. A project: thick again at the end so do some work here, it's worth it; don't rush to complete.

13. Search for the missing link in the project knowledge and history:

a. First, finish what you started, properly and thoroughly to the benefit of everyone.

b. Then document what you know yourself about the project, find out what you don't know about the project and, without shame, ask others what you now need to know to have a fuller understanding.

c. Learn the lessons that are there to be learned and share everything by telling others what you now know.

Be a better project manager (oh, and just ignore all that stuff about dinosaurs, cloaks, psychopaths, creep'o'meters, snow, ballooning, buses, speeches, newspapers and gold – it will probably only confuse you).

Even quicker tips for the really lazy

I'm guessing that size, or the lack of it, really does matter to you…

That seemed to work, I think.

You now have that reference material for future application of the theory of productive laziness. Print it out and stick on your wall and review it each day for inspiration and guidance. Repeat at intervals like a mantra for productive laziness.

What? That seems like too much hard work? Can't we make it any easier? You must be really lazy! (And by 'really lazy' I obviously mean the fast learning, hyper-intelligent, astute students of the book who aspire to almost, but not quite, complete laziness.)

Maybe I can make it easier. Let's see if the logic continues.

What would we get if we applied the 80/20 rule to the 20% that we covered in the previous chapter? I should be now down to just 4% of the wisdom at this point (20% of 20% of 100%, if you are following the maths) and delivering an intense but deeply insightful essence of the whole productive lazy theme. We have moved from fine wine to strong liquor now, quicker to consume and faster to fire the body, so hold on to your hats and grit your teeth.

OK, well, cutting out 80% of the content of the learning points from the preceding chapter and focusing on the remaining 20% gives you this:

1. A project: thick, then thin, then thick again; work hard, rest, work a little – in that order.

2. It is important for you to stay ahead of the game, start confidently, dress appropriately, get the upper hand and anticipate – and keep your eye on the end game.

3. Manage your sponsor, understand them and what they want from you and the project; make sure you know what's in it for them.

4. And manage the project creep, which is inevitable but manageable with a good and proven change process linked to an appreciative use of the parking lot.

5. Avoid communication breakdown through an open and honest effective communication process that suits each individual.

6. Have fun – it will help the project but be careful in your use of fun; encourage a good level of humour amongst the project team.

7. Breathe normally and stay calm, plan for project challenges and when they do happen make sure you filter problems, delegate what you can and prioritise what is left over in order to keep the project on track.

8. Make your project attractive, get the best team and keep them feeling loved by using others on the team together with yourself – and know what love individuals want.

9. Avoid swamping yourself with communication and demands for your time; by all means have an open door, but be a good manager and close it some of the time for the greater good of the project.

10. Always be open to learning more from the project knowledge and history, by talking openly to project team members so that you can learn the lessons that are there to be learned – and share everything by telling others what you now know.

Is that good enough for you now?

Can you afford the extremely minimal time and effort to read this section and potentially commit it to memory? Or at least leave the book open at this page whilst you occasionally glance at it during one of your more active moments?

The ultimate question

It may all end in tears, mark my words, but you know you need to know.

And if that worked, then where will it all end? How far can we go with this process of reduction and simplification?

What is the ultimate answer to life, the universe and productively lazy project management success, in general?

Or, to put it another way, how can you apply the 80/20 rule for the third iteration to distil the very essence of meaning of productive laziness?

Well, if you truly believe in the principles of productive laziness, if you never again want to leave your comfy chair, if you really want your projects to be successful, and if you want to be raised above the heads of your project sponsors and team members in triumphal salute to your sheer brilliance then ... you need to turn the page quickly.

The ultimate answer

Or just three steps to heaven.

Step one: buy a copy of this book for all of your project team members, sponsors, steering committee members, users and subject matter experts – probably best to buy, say, a hundred to be on the safe side.

Step two: get them to all read it thoroughly, or at least read the chapter on 'Even quicker tips for the really lazy'.

Step three: book me as a speaker at the very next opportunity you have and leave the rest to me.

www.thelazyprojectmanager.com

Easy!

Alternatively you could just move to Lazy in Poland.

Łazy		
Coat of arms		
Coordinates:		50°26'N 19°24'E
Country		Poland
Voivodeship		Silesian
County		Zawiercie
Gmina		Łazy
Area		
- Total		8.75 km² (3.4 sq mi)
Population (2006)		
- Total		7,139
- Density		815.9/km² (2,113.1/sq mi)
Postal code		42-450
Website		http://www.lazy.pl/ @

One final word of caution

Success is really defined by what you are looking for.

A project manager was out walking in the countryside one day when a frog called out to her. She bent down, picked up the frog and put it in her pocket. The frog called out again, saying 'If you kiss me I shall turn back into a handsome prince, and I'll stay with you for a week as your lover.' The project manager took the frog out of her pocket, smiled at it and put it back in. The frog called out once more. 'If you kiss me and turn me back into a prince, I'll stay with you for as long as you wish and do absolutely anything that you want.' Again the project manager took the frog out of her pocket, smiled at it and put it back. Finally, the frog demanded 'What's the matter? You can turn me back into a handsome prince, and I'll stay with you forever and do anything you want. Why won't you kiss me?' to which the project manager replied, 'Understand, I'm a project manager. I simply don't have time for a boyfriend, but a talking frog ... that's cool.'

(Of course, not all project managers are female, as I can personally attest, so just reverse the sexes, or not, to suit your own personal point of view or taste.)

And the moral of the story is: if you decide to not become productively lazy – and that is entirely your choice – then you will probably still think a talking frog is cool. And you won't have a need for a nice comfy chair, since you will be far too busy.

Looking forward
to hearing from you

Ladies and gentlemen...

The Lazy Project Manager has now left the building but looks forward to hearing your thoughts and feedback on this book through his website www.thelazyprojectmanager.com

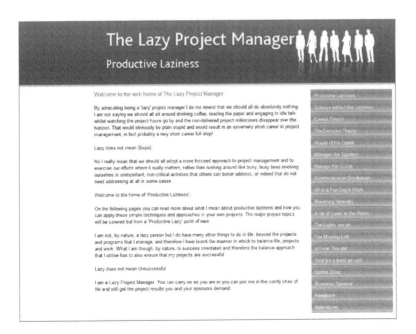

References

Books that the Lazy Project Manager enjoyed reading.

Here are some books that I have enjoyed as sources of information and occasionally education, but these are mostly stuff to read in the comfy chair whilst other people do all the hard work for you.

Brilliant Project Management, Stephen Barker and Rob Cole, Prentice Hall, 2007

Whether you are organising an important event or heading up a large team, running a project can be a daunting process. Project management is fraught with perils; unfinished and unsuccessful projects are everywhere. In fact, it's more common than not for projects to fail. Spiralling costs and missed deadlines are just part of everyday life for many project managers.

But project management doesn't have to be like this. It is possible to manage projects that consistently succeed. *Brilliant Project Management* condenses over thirty years of hands-on project management experience to show you what to do in simple, smart and practical steps.

Project Sponsorship, Randall L. Englund and Alfonso Bucero, Jossey Bass, 2006

This book – which includes case studies, checklists and action plans – shows how project sponsors and project managers can develop the skills they need to manage successful projects. Randall L. Englund and Alfonso Bucero, experts in the field of project management, have written the definitive guide for educating all stakeholders in the nature of project sponsorship. They describe in detail the responsibilities of the project sponsor, from communications and liaison, selection and training, problem solving, mentoring and feedback to the review of project execution. The project sponsor and manager can learn how to negotiate effectively with each other and the project team to achieve their commitments.

The Art of War, Sun Tzu, Filiquarian, 2006

About 2,500 years ago, Sun Tzu wrote this classic book of military strategy based on Chinese warfare and military thought. Since that time, all levels of the military have used the teachings of Sun Tzu on warfare, and they have also been adapted for use in politics, business and everyday life. *The Art of War* is a book which should be used to gain advantage of opponents in the boardroom and battlefield alike. A modern-day interpretation is also available from Karen McCreadie – *The Art of War: A 52 Brilliant Ideas Interpretation*, Infinite Ideas, 2008.

Alpha Project Managers, Andy Crowe, Velociteach, 2006

Debunking misconceptions surrounding successful project managers, this builds on a landmark survey of project managers from around the world to highlight the traits that make them stand out in the minds of their teams, senior managers, customers and stakeholders. Through in-depth interviews and discussions, the common attributes of these elite project managers – from character and beliefs to organisational approaches – are uncovered and help to explain their achievements. Painstakingly researched, this guide offers key insights by providing multiple perspectives on the character of the world's most successful project managers. Andy Crowe is the founder and CEO of Velociteach, a project-management certification business. He is the author of *The PMP Exam: How to Pass on Your First Try*.

That Presentation Sensation, Martin Conradi and Richard Hall, Financial Times/Prentice Hall, 2001

Be good, be clear and be unforgettable... Everyone knows that presentations matter. They make or break ideas and careers. They change minds. They can enhance or destroy value – yours and your company's. But the corporate world is suffering from presentation overload: too many, too dull and too long. It has never been more important to learn the art of commanding attention, of getting your message across so that people remember it – and you. There are hundreds of 'how to' books on presentations. Many are written by people who may have presented in the past (or may not) but who weren't necessarily very good at it. This book is different; it's by the experts, the authors are presentation consultants to the cream of UK companies. Expect ideas, stimulation and tips to make you truly memorable for all the right reasons.

Quick Team Building Activities, Brian Cole Miller, Amacom, 2003

This offers managers simple exercises for team building that don't require special facilities, big expenses or previous training experience. There are lots of useful, practical tasks, well explained, with many suggestions for adapting to day-to-day situations.

The People Side of Project Management, Ralph L. Kliem and Irwin S. Ludin , Gower, 1995

The traditional approach to project management has centred around three criteria – cost, schedule, quality. A fourth is also essential – people. This book looks specifically at the 'people' side, showing how to manage relationships with clients, sponsors and members of the project team itself.

100 Things Project Managers Should Do Before They Die, Rita Mulcahy, RMC Publications, 2008

With all of the craziness that projects usually entail, sometimes we forget to have fun! Did it ever cross your mind to do something a little wacky? Between creating schedules and holding meetings, it is important to make time to enjoy the experiences suggested in this very different kind of to-do list, such as 'Cancel a meeting and see if you really needed it in the first place' and 'Spend a day working from your intuition'. Sections include Getting your point across, Minding the details, Shaping your success, Leading with a new perspective, Creating teamwork and Taking care of you.

Project Retrospectives, Norman L. Kerth, Dorset House, 2001

With detailed scenarios, imaginative illustrations and step-by-step instructions, consultant Norman L. Kerth guides readers through productive, painless retrospectives of project performance. Whether you call them postmortems or postpartums or something else, project retrospectives offer organisations a formal method for preserving the valuable lessons learned from the successes and failures of every project. These lessons and the measurements they yield foster stronger teams and savings on subsequent efforts. For a retrospective to be effective and successful, though, it needs to be safe. Kerth shows facilitators and participants how to defeat the fear of retribution and establish an air of mutual trust.

Applying years of experience as a project retrospective facilitator for software organisations, Kerth reveals his secrets for managing the sensitive, often emotionally charged issues that arise as teams relive and learn from each project. Don't move on to your next project without consulting and using this readable, practical handbook. Each member of your team will be better prepared for the next deadline.

About the author

Ladies and gentlemen, I give you the Lazy Project Manager...

Despite his title of 'The Lazy Project Manager', Peter Taylor is in fact a dynamic and commercially astute professional who has achieved notable success in project management, programme management and the professional development of project managers, latterly as head of projects at a global supplier of performance management system solutions and currently as head of a project management office (PMO) at a global supplier of product lifecycle management solutions.

'And it ought to be remembered that there is nothing more difficult to take in hand, more perilous to conduct, or more uncertain in its success, than to take the lead in the introduction of a new order of things. Because the innovator has for enemies all those who have done well under the old conditions, and lukewarm defenders in those who may do well under the new.

Niccolo Machiavelli, c.1505 (translated W. K. Marriott)

He is an accomplished communicator and leader, always adopting a proactive and business-focused approach. And he is proud to be a successful project manager with a star sign of Virgo (since Virgos clearly make the best project managers).

The Lazy Project Manager can also be persuaded to get out of his really comfortable chair if you feel the need to hear the benefit of his wisdom at your business event.

Project achievements

- Managed over fifty customer projects over a twenty-year period, ranging from departmental solutions to global $10m plus MRP/ERP/CRM and BI/Performance Management projects[35] – as well as a number of internal programmes across Europe, Asia-Pacific and North America.

- Specialised in 'post project' Benefit Realisation and extending the project manager's remit beyond the traditional project close stage.

- Trained and certified in various project management methods.

---

35. Material Requirements Planning (MRP) is a software-based production planning and inventory control system used to manage manufacturing processes. Enterprise resource planning (ERP) is an enterprise-wide information system designed to coordinate all the resources, information and activities needed to complete business processes such as order fulfilment or billing. ERP system supports most of the business system that maintains in a single database the data needed for a variety of business functions such as manufacturing, supply chain management, financials, projects, human resources and customer relationship management (CRM). Business intelligence (BI) refers to skills, knowledge, technologies, applications, quality, risks, security issues and practices used to help a business to acquire a better understanding of market behaviour and commercial context. For this purpose it undertakes the collection, integration, analysis, interpretation and presentation of business information.

- Acted as project management subject matter expert in the development of a number of in-house deployment methodologies.

- Researched and led the investment and development of a project management certification process and operational practice (global >100 project managers).

- Acted as senior advisor in the initiation of a project management office (PMO), focusing on people, process, performance and promotion within a project management centre of excellence.

'Find yourself a nice comfy chair, read this book and then take the lead in the introduction of a new order of things in a productive lazy way.

The Lazy Project Manager, 2009

Index

2249751R00089

Printed in Germany
by Amazon Distribution
GmbH, Leipzig